POSTAL
BAKES

For my granny, Sue.
Your love for baking
proved truly infectious.

PHOTOGRAPHY BY
NASSIMA ROTHACKER

LUCY BURTON

POSTAL
BAKES

OVER 60 CAKES, COOKIES AND OTHER TREATS TO SEND BY MAIL

OH EDITIONS

HOW IT ALL STARTED

There are few topics that I feel informed enough to write a book about but, one global pandemic later, baking and posting delicious modern treats is one of them.

Much as we might like to, 2020 is a year none of us will forget in a hurry. For me – a hospitality PR director with an established side-business making bespoke wedding cakes – the impact of the lockdown restrictions was quick and significant. Almost overnight, the restaurants I represented had closed indefinitely, and a whole season of wedding cake bookings was suddenly postponed or cancelled. With a lot of time on my hands and very little work on my books, I needed to pivot my business and realised that if people couldn't go out to eat cake, I needed to get the cake to them.

I'm often asked where the idea of sending cake in the post came from, but the truth is, I have been making edible presents for as long as I can remember. Growing up, I loved icing biscuits, rolling truffles and making anything that involved getting to use my mum's treasure box of cookie cutters and food colouring. At university, baking was a way of endearing myself to new housemates and later, in my early years in London when money was tight, I'd make batches of jam or salted caramel (page 145) to give as gifts, saving and sterilizing pretty jars throughout the year, and making them that little bit extra special with the addition of a tied ribbon or a hand-stamped label. I'd turn up to house parties with a tub of cookies to make up for the woefully bad wine in my rucksack, and was the least incognito Secret Santa in the office when my recipient unwrapped a box of homemade nougat at the Christmas party.

And so, fuelled by panic and bad Pinot Noir on a drizzly and uncertain evening in March 2020, I plotted out a menu of homemade treats that would be straightforward to make, pack and post. I measured my deep-set baking tins and trawled the internet for boxes that would house the contents snugly. I ordered 50 flatpack white postal boxes – the smallest pack available – and lamented that I'd probably still have most of them kicking around the flat once the 'three-week lockdown' (I know!) was over. I bought cellophane, washi tape, tissue paper and notecards and, deciding that I wanted the boxes to stand out, neon pink packing tape to seal them. The flowers I had so lovingly spent all winter pressing to adorn wedding cakes became my signature postal box decoration instead. I posted the menu on Instagram, and, just like that, a pandemic-friendly baking business was born.

Demand was overwhelming. Any thought of leftover boxes soon evaporated as, thanks to the power of social media, I quickly found myself unable to keep up with orders. My handwritten list of addresses turned into a spreadsheet, wholesale suppliers were quickly found and enlisted, and what had started life as a hashed-together side hustle soon became a highly choreographed business. My spreadsheet had a waiting list and spare boxes (the result of an odd number of orders or, more often, my own disorganisation) were snapped up like, well, hot cakes.

Baking everything out of my then-home kitchen – a light-drenched but bijou galley kitchen in Bermondsey, South London – meant that space was a constant battle. With limited surfaces and oven shelves at my disposal, I had to keep things simple. I offered a weekly changing menu of three or four different items: sometimes cookies, sometimes cake or confectionery, always brownies and blondies. My customers – also stuck in their homes – welcomed the variety, looked forward to the following week's menu, and enjoyed the seasonality of the flavours that I was baking with.

People ordered boxes for their households – their arrival a mini event to look forward to amid the monotony of lockdown – but most ordered for others. As I handwrote every note enclosed

I needed to pivot my business and realised that if people couldn't go out to eat cake, I needed to get the cake to them.

in the boxes, I felt incredibly privileged to share in the love, loss, longing and listlessness that my customers clearly felt. Boxes were being sent to say everything that I was feeling, too – *I love you, I miss you, I'm here for you, We will be together again*. The messages of thanks I received, many from those ordering from overseas or for family far away, were life-affirming and heart-breaking in equal measure. Completely accidentally, I had created a business that was about so much more than baking. It was about reaching out to someone and holding them tight in one of the last remaining ways available to us. Looking back, it was a weird, wild and wonderful time, and just the focus I needed at a time when nothing felt certain.

Thankfully, lockdown is now over for most of us, but seeing the impact and comfort that something as simple as a box of homemade brownies can have is a learning that I plan to carry forward indefinitely. I have built a business out of posting baked goods, which I am not suggesting everyone wants to do. Rather, there are so many times in life where work, study, relationships, travel, illness or clashing diaries separate us from those who we love – and that is what this book is about. I hope the recipes and packaging instructions that follow will inspire you to bake and send treats to the loved ones that you can't see as often as you would like. I think it might surprise you how much it means to them.

While writing this book, I was determined that every recipe in the pages that follow could be baked in the same tin. While there is a time and a place for specialist baking, it brings with it specialist equipment, which is expensive, bulky and – in all honesty – stressful to have around when you are limited on space. Fresh off the bat of running a commercial business out of a small London flat, I have learnt what you need and what you don't need – and the mere thought of a small army of rusting tins that don't stack inside each other neatly is enough to give me a tension headache. I want to change the perception that good baking requires paraphernalia, because frankly, it doesn't.

Whatever your level of culinary prowess, it's likely that you have some form of rectangular oven tray in your kitchen. Whether that's a specialist baking tray, a roasting pan, a pyrex or ceramic cooking dish or simply the tray that came with your oven. Whichever it is, that tray can be used for baking. If you truly don't have any of these things, then you can make one purchase – a 20 x 30 cm (8 x 12 inch) baking tin with deep sides and square corners – and be able to make every recipe in this book. Store it in your oven if needs be, or stack it beneath plates, mugs – whatever. When you're not baking with it, use it to roast a chicken or encase a pasta bake for your dinner.

Many of the recipes in this book are what my mum (and admittedly, many others) would refer to as a traybake. I do not like this name. It is wildly depressing, feels lazy and sounds utterly functional, which these types of treats are most certainly not – but I do love the concept. Time spent in Italy – where desserts are sometimes sliced at the table and served from a rectangular dish – gave my concept of a traybake new energy: traybakes are not only practical but also offer a modern way to create portionable, transportable and, I think, beautiful bakes. Love a traditional teatime slice as I do, there's something fresh and chic about a rectangular slab of cake, simply decorated and neatly cut.

Those recipes that aren't traybakes in the chapters that follow can still be made using the same tin, although the way you use it will differ – flick to page 12 for my suggestions.

INGREDIENTS

Living as we do in a time of mass production and wavering corporate responsibility, it is – I think – important to take the time to know where the ingredients we buy have come from. Where possible, I try to do my research and buy from sustainable and Fairtrade suppliers. If you can, shop locally and follow the seasons – produce is not only better and more affordable when it is at its peak, it also has a much lower carbon footprint. There's also a bit of old-fashioned magic in having to wait for something to come to its best and then when it's gone, it's gone (until next year, anyway).

As shopping in this way is neither quick nor cheap, it can feel like a luxury to dedicate time to these considerations – but if you can, please do. Let's be kind to our planet and support those who are paving the way for looking after it better.

Unless otherwise stated (such as for pastry, when butter should be cold), all ingredients should be brought to room temperature before you begin.

Butter – unsalted and at room temperature, unless otherwise specified.

Dairy – cream should be double (heavy), unless otherwise stated, and full fat. Milk should also be full fat.

Sugars – as you'd expect, these feature heavily in this book. The most commonly used are:

· *Caster (superfine) and golden caster sugar* – mostly interchangeable, though golden will give a richer flavour and slightly deeper hue. For caramels, use regular caster sugar

· *Light brown soft / light muscovado sugar* – for a deep caramel, rich flavour and soft texture

· *Dark brown soft sugar / molasses* – for a deep, almost bitter flavour in heavier bakes

· *Demerara sugar* – toffee flavoured and with a coarser grain that brings texture as well as flavour

· *Icing (confectioner's) sugar* – for glazes and sweetening delicate sponges and biscuits

· *Coconut sugar* – unrefined with a subtle coconut flavour

· *Maple syrup* – a liquid sweetener with a signature flavour

· *Honey* – unrefined and an agent of flavour as well as sweetness

· *Liquid glucose* – inverted and often used in confectionery. Mainly interchangeable with honey, although the latter imparts flavour to bakes

Eggs – medium unless otherwise stated. Free range or organic.

Salt – absolutely essential to season and enhance flavour, and you will find salt in almost every recipe in this book for that reason. I use fine sea salt for flavour, and a flaky salt – such as Maldon – for texture.

Cocoa (unsweetened chocolate) powder – try to find Dutch-process cocoa powder, as it is alkalised and, as such, yields a deeper flavour and brings a beautiful, almost black hue to baked goods.

Chocolate – I tend to use dark chocolate with a minimum of 70% cocoa solids for better flavour. For milk and white varieties, buy what you would eat straight up.

Fruit – for postal bakes, freeze-dried, dried or cooked fruits are required, as fresh fruit has a short shelf life and brings too much moisture to baked goods. All freeze-dried varieties listed in this book are available to purchase from specialist food stores and online. If using fresh produce for a recipe that roasts or bakes the fruit, try and stick to what is in season.

Spices and herbs – dried, unless otherwise stated.

Coconut chips – different to desiccated (dried shredded) coconut, these can be found in bigger supermarkets, health stores or online.

EQUIPMENT

As a city dweller, I have spent years running a baking business out of small galley kitchens and – at the risk of stating the obvious – there simply isn't enough space to keep anything beyond the essentials without slowly losing your mind.

Sick of storing cake tins under my bed, the past few years have seen my kitchen paraphernalia subject to regular and ruthless culls. Most baking can be done with just a few select tools and devices; below are my weapons of choice, and everything you will require to make each and every recipe in this book. When I first moved to London and lived on a shoestring, I bought a lot of my baking equipment in charity shops (or thrift stores), which often have a wide selection of kitchenware. I still check for kitchen and cookbook bargains whenever I stop by.

Oven – all temperatures given in degrees celsius, degrees farenheit and gas mark. If you have a fan oven, decrease the temperature stated by 20°C (68°F). See also the oven thermometer section, below.

Baking tins – every recipe in this book is written to be made in a 20 x 30 cm (8 x 12 inch) rectangular baking tin. If you don't have one, you can follow the tin conversion formula on page 12 to adjust any recipe to fit your tin.

Oven thermometer – you would be amazed how much your actual oven temperature can vary from the number on the dial. An oven thermometer will help you work out whether your oven runs hot or cold, or has hot spots to avoid, and adjust your usage accordingly. I find the type that hangs from the oven shelves easier to read than those that sit in the bottom of the oven.

Digital scales – these are inexpensive and will ensure a much more accurate measurement than analogue scales. Good baking requires precision – a few grams here and there can make all the difference – and digital scales will make this easier.

Sugar thermometer – an essential if you wish to attempt any of the recipes from the confectionery chapter of this book. These are inexpensive and will make sweet-making a lot easier. I prefer digital, but a mercury version will also do the job.

Wire rack – a useful aid for cooling and, if nothing else, somewhere to rest a hot tin.

Stand mixer – I have a KitchenAid stand mixer which is approaching its tenth birthday and still works like new. A mixer of this type is a significant investment but will pay dividends if you bake regularly, not only for the superior results but also because you can get on with other tasks while it is mixing. If you don't have a stand mixer, an electric hand whisk will usually work well. If you don't have one of those, use a wooden spoon for creaming and a hand whisk for whisking – just be prepared for an upper body workout!

Hand whisk – even if you have a stand mixer, this is still an essential tool for making smooth caramels and fruit curds.

Processing and grinding – I use a food processor to grind nuts and oats, mainly for speed, but this is a luxury rather than an essential. If you don't have one, you can chop by hand, but just be aware that it will take a bit longer.

Sieving (straining) – my least favourite job in the kitchen. I will only call for this when it is truly unavoidable. A fine mesh sieve is the most useful type to buy.

Rolling pin – I have a polyethylene rolling pin which I recommend as it is naturally cool and heavy, so does wonders for pastry. If you don't have a rolling pin, an unopened wine bottle will do the job, especially straight out of the fridge.

Spatula – recommended to help get every last drop out of a pan or mixing bowl. Soft plastic ones have the flexibility to get right to the corners, so are much better than hard ones in my opinion.

Ice cream scoop – perfect for evenly portioning and shaping cookie dough. I have a metal one with a squeeze release handle.

Measuring spoons – all tablespoons, teaspoons and fractions thereof are measured in standard industry spoons, and are level unless otherwise stated.

Palette knife – helpful to level surfaces and lift portions from hard-to-reach corners. Always choose off-set variety it you are investing.

Heavy knife – important for slicing neatly. I prefer a sharp edge to a serrated one.

Small serrated fruit knife – useful for preparing fruit quickly.

MISE EN PLACE

My use of the French language starts and finishes with this term, which simply means to have everything 'in its place' before you start making a recipe. This is how professional kitchens operate and, while it can feel like a bit of a performance, this is one of my few prerequisites when teaching anyone to bake.

In layman's terms, to prepare your *mise en place* is to get organised before you start. First, read through the recipe in full to check how long it will take including any resting or infusing times, and to ensure that you have everything you need for the recipe. Next, weigh out your ingredients, complete any prep jobs like chopping or zesting, preheat the oven and line your tin. Once all of these jobs are done, you can start to actually make the recipe.

Following this method while in a kitchen ensures that when you come to start baking, you have exactly what you need to hand. Believe me, taking this first step will make the process quicker.

HOW TO LINE YOUR TIN

Most of the recipes in this book require the tin to be lined with baking parchment (or greaseproof paper) to ensure the contents do not stick and can be easily removed once cooked. There are two methods of lining specified – with sides, and without.

For cookies, biscuits and confectionery, you generally don't need to line the sides, as the contents of the tin won't touch them. For these recipes, simply cut a piece of paper wide enough to comfortably fit the base of the tin, making sure the edges aren't hanging loose, as these have a tendency to flap around during baking and fall onto whatever is in the tin.

For traybakes (brownies, blondies, bars and cakes), you need to line the sides of the tins, too. I do this by eye, cutting a piece wide enough to give you two long sides as well as the base. Four quick snips with a pair of scissors allow you to neatly create corners and four sides, and the sheet can then be lifted into the tin.

A few of the confectionery recipes will call for a cling film (plastic wrap) lining instead of baking parchment. I try to avoid single-use plastic but am yet to find a sustainable alternative that works as well in this scenario. When cling film is called for, double-line the tin with two wide sheets, allowing plenty of overhang to help you lift the goods out when they are set.

TIN CONVERSION

The easiest way to scale a recipe down to fit the tin you are using is to follow this formula. Place your tin on a set of digital scales, set to zero, then fill with water to just below the brim. The weight = **x**.

The 20 x 30 cm (8 x 12 inch) tin which these recipes are designed to fit has a volume of 2,100 g. Divide **x** by 2100 and note down that number (**y**). When you come to make a recipe, you just need to multiply each ingredient quantity by **y** to scale the recipe down to fit your tin. Here's an example:

*The water weighed into the new tin is 1,500 g (**x**). 1500 (**x**) divided by 2,100 = 0.71 (**y**). To scale the recipe, multiply each ingredient quantity by 0.71 to adjust to the correct quantity.*

You will need to use your common sense to ensure the recipe works (e.g. you can't use 0.71 of an egg) and note that a smaller batch is likely to take less time to bake, so check it frequently.

This method of scaling down the recipes only works for those using metric (gram) measurements. For those more used to using imperial (ounce) or cup measurements, your digital scales should easily flick between metric and imperial, so why not give metric a try if you want to scale down a recipe.

For traybakes, line the sides as well as the base.

For cookies and biscuits you don't need to line the sides.

A few confectionery recipes call for double lining with cling film. Allow plenty of overhang.

HOW TO POST BAKED ITEMS

Posting bars, cakes, cookies and confectionery is easier than you think, and every recipe in this book has been written specifically to ensure that it is up to the journey. To ensure your creations travel well, there are two main considerations: how you wrap and pack your items, and the shelf life you are working with.

SHELF LIFE

I haven't included any recipes for items that have too short a shelf life – like bread doughs – or anything too delicate – like meringues – for the very purpose of ensuring that you don't need to worry about these things. There are no elements that require fridge storage, such as fresh cream, for obvious reasons.

That said, there are a range of shelf lives detailed in this book, so please check the recipe you plan to make before you post it, to ensure that it is fit for purpose. You will then need to select your method of postage based on the shelf life. Items with shorter shelf lives (up to a week) should be sent using next-day delivery services, while items with longer shelf lives like brownies and blondies can be sent using standard delivery.

PACKAGING

These packaging recommendations are based on my experience of operating a business sending bars, cakes and cookies in the post. This is not to say that this is the only way to do it, but I can confirm that this method works.

Step 1: Choosing your box

The key to ensuring that items travel safely is to post them in a box as close in size to the wrapped item as possible. Empty space facilitates movement in transit, and it is movement which can lead to breakages and squashing. If an item can't move, it will travel beautifully. See my notes at Step 5 on how to approach mixed boxes and empty spaces.

I have only ever sent treats in a box and would not recommend using a jiffy bag (even if padded internally), as the latter has no strong walls to protect the contents.

If you are using the 20 x 30 cm (8 x 12 inch) tin, half of that slab will fit perfectly, once wrapped, into a 21.5 x 15.5 x 5 cm (8½ x 6 x 2 inch) box, or a quarter into a 18 x 10 x 5 cm (7 x 4 x 2 inch) box. Please note that neither of these sized boxes will fit through a regular letter box, so it's worth warning your recipient that they are expecting a parcel!

Step 2: Food-safe cellophane or baking parchment

To ensure your items stay fresh and are safe to eat, the first step of packaging is to wrap them tightly and securely. I use food-safe cellophane but you can also use baking parchment. I cut bars and cakes into slabs (either portioned or left whole), to be wrapped in a secure rectangular shape. Cookies and biscuits should be packed tightly in either a cylinder (for round biscuits) or in a small cellophane or greaseproof paper bag. Seal all wrapping tightly using masking (washi) tape.

At this stage, I like to add a small sticker with a best-before date to ensure the recipient knows how long the treats will last for.

Step 3: Tissue paper

Wrapping your cellophaned goods generously in tissue paper adds an extra layer of cushion and protection.

I use at least two layers of tissue and a big enough sheet to ensure there is extra tissue paper at the sides which, when folded down neatly, will offer extra cushioning. You can also use fabrics like cotton, linen or muslin, if you prefer.

Step 4: Ribbon or string
This is predominantly decorative, but a tied ribbon or string also helps to hold everything in place, adding extra protection.

Step 5: Packing the box
Once your baked goods are all wrapped, it's time to pack the box. If you are sending a mixed box, place heavier slabs at the bottom and cookies and biscuits on top. If you have any empty spaces, scrunch up extra tissue paper into balls and use it to fill the spaces neatly. You could also use shredded tissue paper or wood wool.

Step 6: Decoration
Top the box with your chosen decorations and notecard.

Step 7: Seal and address
Seal the box with parcel tape, address and post using a service appropriate to the shelf life of the contents.

DECORATION AND INCLUSIONS

Once you've packed your treats to ensure they travel safely, it's up to you how you decorate the boxes. I like to keep the styling simple, but ensure it is thoughtful and coherent. Here are some suggestions of items to use to finish your boxes:

- A handwritten notecard, enclosed in a beautiful envelope, to prolong the unwrapping process

- Ribbons – silk, organza, taffeta and velvet all work well – or baker's twine

- Pressed and dried flowers and petals (page 146)

- Candles for birthdays, which can be tucked beneath the ribbon or taped in place with washi tape, and mini match packets or jars

- Biodegradable confetti

- Flower or herb seed packets

- Homemade tea blends and muslin bags, with a mini tea strainer included

- Ground coffee, with a little teaspoon attached

STORAGE

While none of these recipes include any elements that require fridge storage, treats can get a little warm in transit in the summer months. I recommend including a best before date on everything you send (see each recipe for guidance on shelf life), and a note suggesting that the recipient stores them in the fridge for a couple of hours to firm up before serving.

ALLERGENS

It's important that your recipients know exactly what is inside the goodies you send them, so I recommend writing out the ingredients on a card and enclosing it in the parcel. Be particularly sure to note whether the bakes include gluten, dairy, nuts, egg and sesame. If you plan to sell any food items (posted or not), be sure to check the legal requirements in your market for food labelling, safety and hygiene.

This card is also a good place to note how long the items will keep for, and how they should be stored. All items should be stored at room temperature (although as noted above, may benefit from a quick spell in the fridge during hot weather) in airtight containers or packaging.

BROWNIES
+
BLONDIES

BROWNIES

Salted Caramel
Stem Ginger + Sour Cherry
Sticky Toffee
Rose + Raspberry
Mulled Wine
Peppermint
Stout + Vanilla Cream
PBJ
Salted Almond
Hazelnut Ripple + White Chocolate
Kids' Party

BLONDIES

Raspberry Ripple + Brown Butter
Apricot + Almond
Blackcurrant + Caramelised White Chocolate
Banoffee
Hazelnut + Dark Chocolate Splatter
Matcha
Strawberry, Rhubarb + Custard
Pistachio Praline
Passionfruit + Coconut
Eggnog

THE RECIPES IN THIS CHAPTER WERE THE FOUNDATIONS OF MY POSTAL BAKES BUSINESS.

Each of the ideas that follow uses one of two simple base recipes – a brownie and a blondie – through which seasonal curds, caramels, jams, custards and nut pastes are swirled, and toppings are scattered over either before or after baking. The flavour options are endless really, but these are some of my favourites.

SALTED CARAMEL BROWNIES

PREP: 15 minutes, plus chilling and making the salted caramel
COOK: 30–40 minutes
MAKES: 16 bars
or 24 smaller squares

FOR THE BROWNIE BATTER:

300 g (10½ oz) unsalted butter, cubed

400 g (14 oz/1¾ cups) caster (superfine) sugar

100 g (3½ oz/generous ½ cup) light brown soft sugar

70 g (2½ oz/generous ½ cup) cocoa (unsweetened chocolate) powder

70 g (2½ oz) dark chocolate (minimum 70% cocoa solids) chopped into small pieces

4 eggs

140 g (5 oz/generous 1 cup) plain (all-purpose) flour

½ tsp fine sea salt

FOR THE TOPPING:

100 g (3½ oz) salted caramel (page 145)

flaky sea salt, for sprinkling

NOTES

SHELF LIFE: All of the brownies in this book will last for at least two weeks when tightly wrapped in airtight packaging.

HOW TO POST: Wrap tightly in cellophane and tissue paper. These can be sent as part of a mixed box (and are robust enough to sit at the bottom) or in a well-fitted box.

Sending box after box of brownies through the post was the inspiration for this book, and my quest to develop the perfect recipe has been a long one. I have tried countless ratios of butter, sugar and flour; baking temperatures (hot and fast, low and slow); and cocoa agents (dark chocolate – if so, what percentage of cocoa – or cocoa powder, or both). Finally, I feel confident that I have one of the best brownie recipes out there.

These are densely chocolatey, but also slice beautifully and, thanks to the two sugars used in the recipe, have a perfectly crisp, meringue-like crust.

Preheat the oven to 180°C (350°F/gas mark 6) and line a 20 x 30 cm (8 x 12 inch) tin following the instructions on page 12.

To make the brownie batter, put the butter in a large saucepan followed by the caster sugar, brown sugar, cocoa powder and dark chocolate (it is important to put the ingredients in the pan in this order, so that the butter melts first). Place the pan over a low heat and leave for 5 minutes, without stirring, until the butter has completely melted and enveloped the other ingredients. After 5 minutes, give the mixture a stir with a whisk to bring everything together. Once the butter and chocolate are fully melted, remove the pan from the heat (don't worry if the sugar is still slightly granular at this point).

Crack the eggs directly into the pan, then quickly whisk the mixture together until it is glossy and all the ingredients are fully incorporated. Add the flour and salt to the pan and whisk again briefly, until just combined. Make sure you get into the corners of the pan with the whisk to catch any pockets of flour which haven't been mixed through. Pour the mixture into your lined tin, gently tilting the tin to encourage the mixture to fill to the edges in an even layer.

To top the brownie, use 2 teaspoons to dollop spoonfuls of the salted caramel evenly over the surface of the brownie mixture, then use a toothpick to ripple the caramel through the batter. Sprinkle the surface of the brownie with a pinch of flaky sea salt.

Place the tin in the centre of the oven and bake for 30–40 minutes, until the brownie no longer wobbles when lightly shaken and a skewer inserted into the middle comes out with just a few wet crumbs.

Allow the brownie to cool to room temperature in the tin, then place in the fridge for an hour before slicing. (This will help you get clean edges when you slice the brownies.) Once the brownie has cooled, remove from the tin and slice into 16 brownie bars or 24 smaller squares, if you prefer.

OTHER BROWNIE IDEAS

One of my favourite parts of running my postal cakes business is thinking up and developing new and exciting flavour combinations to bake into the hundreds of trays of brownies and blondies that I make each week. Those on the following pages are some old favourites, which my customers might just recognise, alongside a few new ideas that were developed especially for this book.

Each of the following brownie recipes uses the same brownie batter used in my Salted Caramel Brownies (page 23) before different toppings and flavours are added. The shelf life and postage recommendations remain the same.

STEM GINGER + SOUR CHERRY BROWNIES

PREP: 15 minutes, plus chilling
COOK: 30–40 minutes
MAKES: 16 bars or
24 smaller squares

1 x quantity brownie batter
(page 23)

FOR THE TOPPING:
75 g (2½ oz) stem ginger,
cut into 1 cm (½ inch) cubes

20 g (¾ oz) dried or freeze-dried
sour cherries

flaky sea salt, for sprinkling

*With the sweet heat of ginger and tang of sour cherry, this is
a grown-up brownie. A handful of candied citrus peel is a welcome
and bright addition and can be added at the same time as the ginger.*

Preheat the oven to 180°C (350°F/gas mark 6) and line a 20 x 30 cm
(8 x 12 inch) tin following the instructions on page 12.

Make the brownie batter following the recipe and method for the
Salted Caramel Brownies (page 23), omitting the salted caramel, and
pouring the batter into your prepared tin and levelling out the surface
in the same way.

To top the brownie, scatter the cubes of stem ginger over the
surface of the brownie as evenly as you can, using the back of a
teaspoon to gently push them down and smooth the batter over them.
If you are using dried cherries, scatter these over the surface of the
brownie now; if you are using freeze-dried cherries, set aside until after
the brownies are baked (see below). Sprinkle with a pinch of flaky sea salt.

Bake the brownies as per the recipe on page 23. If you are using
freeze-dried cherries, scatter them over the brownie as soon as it is
removed from the oven, then use the back of the spoon to gently press
the cherries down into the surface. Chill and slice your brownies as per
the recipe on page 23.

STICKY TOFFEE BROWNIES

PREP: 15 minutes, plus chilling
and making the salted caramel
COOK: 30–40 minutes
MAKES: 16 bars
or 24 smaller squares

1 x quantity brownie batter
(page 23)

FOR THE TOPPING:
75 g (2½ oz) salted caramel
(page 145)

50 g (2 oz/generous ¼ cup) dates,
stoned and roughly chopped

30 g (1 oz/ generous ¼ cup) pecans,
roughly chopped

flaky sea salt, for sprinkling

*I'm rarely one to trifle with a classic, but what's not to love here?
One of the most perfect desserts, imbued in a brownie. While not
strictly traditional, I like to add a sprinkling of chopped pecans
for a little extra texture.*

Preheat the oven to 180°C (350°F/gas mark 6) and line a 20 x 30 cm
(8 x 12 inch) tin following the instructions on page 12.

Make the brownie batter following the recipe on page 23,
pouring the batter into your prepared tin, levelling out the surface
and dotting over the salted caramel in the same way. Scatter the
dates and pecans evenly over the surface of the brownie batter, then
sprinkle over some salt.

Bake, chill and slice the brownies as per the recipe on page 23.

ROSE + RASPBERRY BROWNIES

PREP: 15 minutes, plus chilling
COOK: 30–40 minutes
MAKES: 16 bars
or 24 smaller squares

1 x quantity brownie batter
(page 23)

2 tsp rose water

flaky sea salt to top

100g Turkish Delight

30g freeze dried raspberries

crystallised rose petals to finish
(optional, recipe on page 146)

FOR THE TOPPING:
100 g (3½ oz) Turkish delight,
cut into 2cm (1 inch) cubes

flaky sea salt, for sprinkling

30 g (1 oz) freeze-dried raspberries

Berries and florals are a long-lauded pairing, with the delicate perfume of rose standing up to the sharpness of raspberries. If rose flavour isn't for you, swap the Turkish delight for a scattering of pistachio slivers and omit the rose water.

Preheat the oven to 180°C (350°F/gas mark 6) and line a 20 x 30 cm (8 x 12 inch) tin following the instructions on page 12.

Make the brownie batter following the recipe and method for the Salted Caramel Brownies (page 23), omitting the salted caramel, and whisking the rose water through the batter before pouring it into your prepared tin and levelling out the surface. Sprinkle with a pinch of flaky sea salt.

Bake the brownie as per the recipe on page 23. As soon as the brownie is removed from the oven, scatter the Turkish delight and freeze-dried raspberries and a handful of crystallised rose petals over the top, then use the back of the spoon to gently press the toppings down into the surface. Chill and slice your brownies as per the recipe on page 23.

MULLED WINE CHRISTMAS BROWNIES

PREP: 30 minutes, plus chilling
COOK: 30–40 minutes
MAKES: 16 bars
or 24 smaller squares

1 x quantity brownie batter
(page 23)

FOR THE MULLED WINE:
200 ml (7 fl oz/scant 1 cup) red wine

1 cinnamon stick

2 cardamom pods

4 cloves

1 vanilla pod, cut in half lengthways

pared zest of 1 orange

I developed and tested this recipe during my first winter in London. If you prefer, you can remove the wine and instead heat 100 g (3.5 oz) of salted caramel with the spices for 15–20 minutes to infuse before rippling through the brownies. This is the original version – which my friends talk about to this day – and I think is still my favourite.

Preheat the oven to 180°C (350°F/gas mark 6) and line a 20 x 30 cm (8 x 12 inch) tin following the instructions on page 12.

To make the mulled wine, put all the ingredients in a small pan and bring to a simmer over a low heat until the wine has reduced in volume by half. Set aside to cool to room temperature, then remove and discard the the spices and orange zest.

Make the brownie batter following the recipe on page 23, omitting the caramel, and whisking the cooled mulled wine through the brownie batter before pouring it into your prepared tin and levelling out the surface.

Bake, chill and slice the brownies as per the recipe on page 23.

PEPPERMINT CHRISTMAS BROWNIES

PREP: 15 minutes, plus chilling
COOK: 30–40 minutes
MAKES: 16 bars
or 24 smaller squares

100 g (3½ oz) mint thin chocolates

1 x quantity brownie batter
(page 23)

25 g (1 oz) candy canes

These form part of my Christmas postal range and – topped with a sprinkling of pale pink and green crushed candy canes – make for the prettiest festive treat.

Preheat the oven to 180°C (350°F/gas mark 6) and line a 20 x 30 cm (8 x 12 inch) tin following the instructions on page 12.

Break the mint thins into small pieces and spread over the base of your prepared tin in an even layer. Make the brownie batter following the recipe on page 23, pouring the batter into your prepared tin over the mint thins, levelling out the surface and baking in the same way, but omitting the salted caramel topping stage.

While the brownie is baking, put the candy canes in a food-safe bag and bash with a rolling pin until well crumbled. As soon as the brownie is removed from the oven, scatter the crushed candy cane pieces over the top in an even layer and push gently into the surface of the brownies. Chill and slice your brownies as per the recipe on page 23.

STOUT + VANILLA CREAM BROWNIES

PREP: 15 minutes, plus chilling
COOK: 30–40 minutes
MAKES: 16 bars
or 24 smaller squares

1 x quantity brownie batter
(page 23)
100 ml (3½ fl oz/scant ½ cup) stout

FOR THE TOPPING:
150 g (5 oz/scant ¾ cup) mascarpone
10 g (½ oz) icing (confectioner's)
sugar
1 tsp vanilla extract

Stout and cocoa are a marriage made in heaven, and a thick ripple of vanilla-speckled, slightly sweetened mascarpone makes the union all the sweeter.

Preheat the oven to 180°C (350°F/gas mark 6) and line a 20 x 30 cm (8 x 12 inch) tin following the instructions on page 12.

Make the brownie batter following the recipe on page 23, omitting the caramel, and whisking the stout through the brownie batter before pouring it into your prepared tin and levelling out the surface.

Beat the mascarpone, icing sugar and vanilla extract together in a small bowl until smooth and well combined.

Use 2 teaspoons to dot the mascarpone mixture over the surface of the brownie, then use a toothpick to ripple it through the batter.

Bake, chill and slice the brownies as per the recipe on page 23.

PBJ BROWNIES

PREP: 15 minutes, plus chilling
COOK: 30–40 minutes
MAKES: 16 bars
or 24 smaller squares

1 x quantity brownie batter
(page 23)

FOR THE TOPPING:
75 g (2½ oz/scant ⅓ cup)
crunchy peanut butter
75 g (2½ oz/generous ¼ cup)
strawberry jam
25 g (1 oz) smooth peanut butter
(optional)
flaky sea salt, for sprinkling

A classic combination which needs little introduction. I like to ripple smooth peanut butter across the surface of the brownie and spoon dollops of a thicker, crunchy variety to create pockets within the baked brownie crumb.

Preheat the oven to 180°C (350°F/gas mark 6) and line a 20 x 30 cm (8 x 12 inch) tin following the instructions on page 12.

Make the brownie batter following the recipe on page 23, omitting the caramel, and pouring the batter into your prepared tin and levelling out the surface in the same way.

To top the brownie, use 2 teaspoons to dot the crunchy peanut butter over the surface of the batter, then repeat with the strawberry jam. Using a clean teaspoon, push the peanut butter and jam down into the brownie, smoothing the batter over the top. If you are using the smooth peanut butter, warm it slightly in the microwave until it reaches a drizzling consistency, then drizzle it evenly over the brownie. Ripple the smooth peanut butter through the surface of the batter with a toothpick, then sprinkle with a little flaky sea salt.

Bake, chill and slice the brownies as per the recipe on page 23.

SALTED ALMOND BROWNIES

PREP: 15 minutes, plus chilling
COOK: 30–40 minutes
MAKES: 16 bars
or 24 smaller squares

1 x quantity brownie batter
(page 23)

FOR THE TOPPING:
50 g (2 oz) almond butter

50 g (2 oz/⅓ cup) whole,
skin-on almonds

25 g (1 oz/¼ cup) flaked
(slivered) almonds

flaky sea salt, for sprinkling

Enriched with three forms of almonds, these brownies were inspired by Panforte, a deliciously chewy Italian dessert that is usually served at Christmas.

Preheat the oven to 180°C (350°F/gas mark 6) and line a 20 x 30 cm (8 x 12 inch) tin following the instructions on page 12.

Make the brownie batter following the recipe on page 23, omitting the caramel, and pouring the batter into your prepared tin and levelling out the surface in the same way.

To top the brownie, use 2 teaspoons to dot the almond butter over the surface, then use a toothpick to ripple it through the batter. Scatter the whole almonds over the surface of the brownie, followed by the flaked almonds. You want the nuts to sit on the surface, so do not push them down into the batter. Sprinkle with a pinch of flaky sea salt.

Bake, chill and slice the brownies as per the recipe on page 23.

HAZELNUT RIPPLE + WHITE CHOCOLATE BROWNIES

PREP: 15 minutes, plus chilling
COOK: 30–40 minutes
MAKES: 16 bars
or 24 smaller squares

1 x quantity brownie batter
(page 23)

FOR THE TOPPING:
50 g (2 oz) hazelnut paste

75g (2½ oz) white chocolate,
roughly chopped

50g (2 oz/generous ⅓ cup)
hazelnuts, blanched or skin on,
roughly chopped

The addition of smooth puréed hazelnut and sweet white chocolate was inspired, I think, by a well-loved breakfast spread – and these brownies are every bit as delicious as their muse.

Preheat the oven to 180°C (350°F/gas mark 6) and line a 20 x 30 cm (8 x 12 inch) tin following the instructions on page 12.

Make the brownie batter following the recipe on page 23, omitting the caramel, and pouring the batter into your prepared tin and levelling out the surface in the same way.

To top the brownie, use 2 teaspoons to dot the hazelnut paste over the surface, then use a toothpick to ripple it through the batter. Scatter the white chocolate over the surface of the brownie, using the back of a spoon to press the chocolate down into the batter slightly. Finally, scatter over the chopped hazelnuts, but let these sit on the surface rather than pressing them down.

Bake, chill and slice the brownies as per the recipe on page 23.

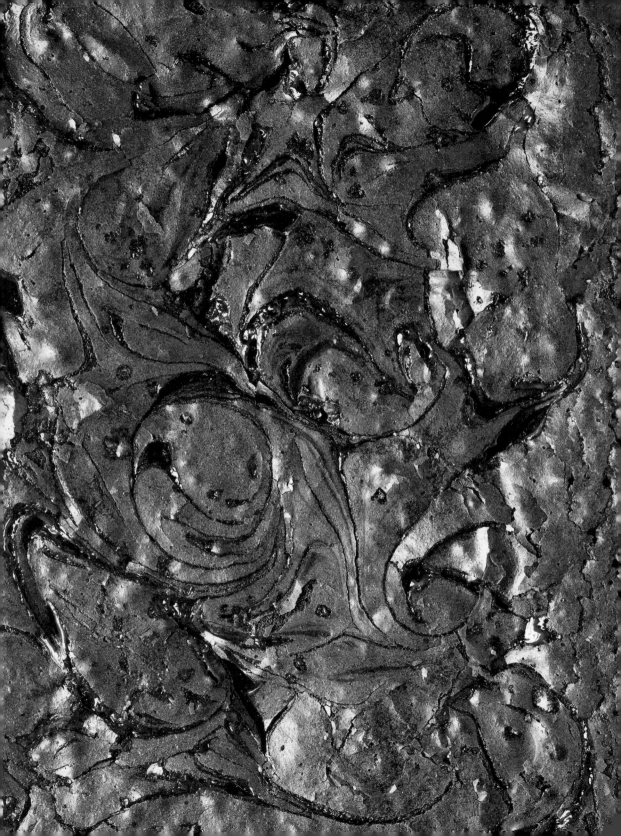

KIDS' PARTY BROWNIES

PREP: 15 minutes, plus chilling
COOK: 30–40 minutes
MAKES: 16 bars
or 24 smaller squares

1 x quantity brownie batter
(page 23)

100 g (3½ oz) biscuits and/or
sweets of your choice

These brownies couldn't be simpler to make, and are sure to delight kids big and small. Load them up with your favourite party biscuits, sweets and sprinkles.

Preheat the oven to 180°C (350°F/gas mark 6) and line a 20 x 30 cm (8 x 12 inch) tin following the instructions on page 12.

Make the brownie batter following the recipe on page 23, omitting the caramel, and pouring the batter into your prepared tin, levelling out the surface and baking in the same way.

As soon as the brownie is removed from the oven, add the biscuits and sweets. Start with the bigger biscuits, then fill in any gaps with broken biscuit pieces and smaller sweets. Use the back of the spoon to gently press the biscuits and/or sweets down into the surface of the brownie, then chill and slice as per the recipe on page 23.

RASPBERRY RIPPLE + BROWN BUTTER BLONDIES

PREP: 20 minutes, plus cooling and making the raspberry curd
COOK: 35–40 minutes
MAKES: 16 bars
or 24 smaller squares

FOR THE BLONDIE BATTER:

300 g (10½ oz) unsalted butter, cubed

3 eggs

175 g (6 oz/¾ cup) caster (superfine) sugar

200 g (7 oz/1 cup) light brown soft sugar

350 g (12 oz/scant 3 cups) plain (all-purpose) flour

1½ tsp fine sea salt

FOR THE TOPPING:

100 g (3½ oz) raspberry curd (see page 140) or shop-bought seedless raspberry jam

100 g (3½ oz) white chocolate, roughly chopped

10 g (½ oz) freeze-dried raspberries

NOTES

SHELF LIFE: All of the blondie recipes in this book will keep well for two weeks when wrapped in airtight packaging.

SUBSTITUTIONS: There are plenty of ideas for different ingredients to use in your blondies in the pages that follow. For this recipe, you could swap the raspberries for another freeze-dried berry, or the white chocolate for a darker blend.

HOW TO POST: Wrap tightly in cellophane and tissue paper. These can be sent as part of a mixed box or in a well-fitted box.

During the lockdowns of 2020 and 21, these blondies were one of the most ordered items for my postal bakes business. Browning the butter used in the blondie base imparts a nutty, caramel flavour which offsets the sharpness of raspberry ripple perfectly. You can make your own raspberry curd (page 140) or substitute for the same amount of shop-bought seedless raspberry jam, if you prefer.

Preheat the oven to 160°C (320°F/gas mark 4) and line a 20 x 30 cm (8 x 12 inch) tin following the instructions on page 12.

To make the blondie batter, melt the butter in a small pan over a low heat, then turn up the heat to medium-high and leave to bubble and foam until the milk solids turn golden brown. Remove from the heat and set aside to cool slightly.

Crack the eggs into a large mixing bowl or the bowl of a stand mixer and add both types of sugar. Using an electric whisk or the whisk attachment of the stand mixer, whisk the eggs and sugar for 4–5 minutes until fluffy, light and airy. With the whisk still running, slowly pour in the brown butter, continuing to whisk until the mixture is well incorporated and glossy. Add the flour and salt to the bowl and gently fold into the mixture until smooth. Pour the mixture into your lined tin, gently tilting the tin to encourage the mixture to fill to the edges in an even layer.

To top the blondie, use 2 teaspoons to dot the raspberry curd or jam over the surface, then use a toothpick to ripple it through the batter. Scatter the chopped white chocolate evenly over the top of the blondie, then transfer to the oven to bake for 35–40 minutes, until the surface is golden and no longer wobbles when gently shaken.

As soon as the blondie is removed from the oven, scatter the freeze-dried raspberries over the top, then use the back of the spoon to gently press the raspberries down into the surface.

Allow the blondie to cool to room temperature, then remove from the tin and slice into 16 bars or 24 smaller squares, if you prefer.

OTHER
BLONDIE IDEAS

Blondies are the perfect base to get creative
with flavours. They work beautifully spiked with
fruit, caramel, chocolate, nuts, or anything else
you can think of! The following recipes are a mix
of combinations old and new that I've loved
baking, posting and (most importantly) eating.

Each of the blondie recipes in this book features
the brown butter blondie batter used in my
Raspberry Ripple + Brown Butter Blondies
recipe (page 38), before different toppings
and flavours are added. The shelf life and
postage recommendations remain the same.

APRICOT + ALMOND BLONDIES

PREP: 20 minutes, plus cooling
COOK: 35–40 minutes
MAKES: 16 bars
or 24 smaller squares

1 x quantity blondie batter
(page 38)

FOR THE TOPPING:
75 g (2½ oz/scant ¼ cup) apricot jam

75g (2½ oz) almond paste

25 g (1 oz/¼ cup) flaked (slivered)
almonds

10 g (½ oz) freeze-dried apricots

Pastries filled with sweet jammy apricots and almond paste inspired this idea. If you can't find almond paste, finely diced marzipan works beautifully instead.

Preheat the oven to 160°C (320°F/gas mark 4) and line a 20 x 30 cm (8 x 12 inch) tin following the instructions on page 12.

Make the blondies following the recipe on page 38, pouring the batter into your prepared tin, levelling out the surface and baking in the same way, but omitting the topping stages.

To top the blondie, use 2 teaspoons to dot the apricot jam over the surface, then use a toothpick to ripple it through the batter. Crumble the almond paste over the batter evenly. Scatter the flaked almonds on top.

As soon as the blondie is removed from the oven, scatter the freeze-dried apricots over the top, then use the back of the spoon to gently press them down into the surface. Cool and slice the blondies as per the recipe on page 38.

BLACKCURRANT + CARAMELISED WHITE CHOCOLATE BLONDIES

PREP: 20 minutes, plus making
the caramelised white chocolate
and cooling
COOK: 35–40 minutes
MAKES: 16 bars
or 24 smaller squares

1 x quantity blondie batter
(page 38)

FOR THE TOPPING:
75 g (2½ oz/scant ¼ cup)
blackcurrant jam

100 g (3½ oz) caramelised
white chocolate (page 123),
roughly chopped

10 g (½ oz) freeze-dried blackcurrants

Perfect for late summer when blackcurrants burst into season, these blondies have just the right amount of tart filling to balance the golden caramelised white chocolate.

Preheat the oven to 160°C (320°F/gas mark 4) and line a 20 x 30 cm (8 x 12 inch) tin following the instructions on page 12.

Make the blondie batter following the recipe on page 38, pouring the batter into your prepared tin and levelling out the surface in the same way, but omitting the toppings.

To top the blondie, use 2 teaspoons to dot the blackcurrant jam over the surface, then use a toothpick to ripple it through the batter. Scatter over the caramelised white chocolate pieces. Bake the blondie as per the recipe on page 38.

As soon as the blondie is removed from the oven, scatter the freeze-dried blackcurrants over the top, then use the back of the spoon to gently press them down into the surface. Cool and slice the blondies as per the recipe on page 38.

BANOFFEE BLONDIES

PREP: 20 minutes, plus making the salted caramel and cooling
COOK: 35–40 minutes
MAKES: 16 bars
or 24 smaller squares

1 x quantity blondie batter
(page 38)

FOR THE TOPPING:
75 g (2½ oz) salted caramel
(page 145)

50 g (2 oz) dried banana,
roughly chopped

50 g (2 oz) dark chocolate (minimum
70% cocoa solids), roughly chopped

10 g (½ oz) freeze-dried banana slices

Bananas feature in some of the world's finest sweet recipes, and – I think – these blondies are no exception to that loosely formed rule. I like to add a scattering of bitter dark chocolate to balance the sweeter ingredients.

Preheat the oven to 160°C (320°F/gas mark 4) and line a 20 x 30 cm (8 x 12 inch) tin following the instructions on page 12.

Make the blondie batter following the recipe on page 38, omitting the toppings, pouring the batter into your prepared tin and levelling out the surface in the same way.

To top the blondie, use 2 teaspoons to dot the salted caramel over the surface, then use a toothpick to ripple it through the batter. Scatter the chopped dried banana and the dark chocolate evenly over the top, then bake as per the recipe on page 38.

As soon as the blondie is removed from the oven, scatter over the freeze-dried banana slices, then use the back of the spoon to gently press them down into the surface. Cool and slice the blondies as per the recipe on page 38.

HAZELNUT + DARK CHOCOLATE SPLATTER BLONDIES

PREP: 20 minutes, plus making the salted caramel and cooling
COOK: 35–40 minutes
MAKES: 16 bars
or 24 smaller squares

1 x quantity blondie batter
(page 38)

FOR THE TOPPING:
75 g (2½ oz) salted caramel
(page 145)

50 g (2½ oz) chocolate hazelnut
spread

50 g (2½ oz/generous ⅓ cup)
hazelnuts, roughly chopped

50 g (2½ oz) dark chocolate
(minimum 70% cocoa solids),
roughly chopped

Scattered with coarsely chopped dark chocolate before going into the oven, these blondies have a beautiful mottled finish once baked.

Preheat the oven to 160°C (320°F/gas mark 4) and line a 20 x 30 cm (8 x 12 inch) tin following the instructions on page 12.

Make the blondie batter following the recipe on page 38, omitting the toppings, pouring the batter into your prepared tin and levelling out the surface in the same way.

To top the blondie, use 2 teaspoons to dot the salted caramel over the surface, followed by the chocolate hazelnut spread, then use a toothpick to ripple them through the batter. Scatter the chopped hazelnuts and dark chocolate evenly over the top, then bake, cool and slice as per the recipe on page 38.

MATCHA BLONDIES

PREP: 20 minutes, plus cooling
COOK: 35–40 minutes
MAKES: 16 bars
or 24 smaller squares

1 x quantity blondie batter
(page 38)

10 g (½ oz) matcha powder

FOR THE TOPPING:
75 g (2½ oz) white chocolate,
roughly chopped

25 g (1 oz) shelled pistachios,
roughly chopped

Thanks to its savoury flavour and verdant hue, the addition of matcha makes for blondies with a difference. I love the slightly bitter note the matcha brings to the blondie batter, which pairs perfectly with white chocolate and fragrant pistachios.

Preheat the oven to 160°C (320°F/gas mark 4) and line a 20 x 30 cm (8 x 12 inch) tin following the instructions on page 12.

Make the blondie batter following the recipe on page 38, omitting the toppings, and adding the matcha powder at the same time as the flour, then pouring the batter into your prepared tin and levelling out the surface in the same way. Scatter the chopped white chocolate and pistachios evenly over the surface of the blondie, then bake, cool and slice as per the recipe on page 38.

STRAWBERRY, RHUBARB + CUSTARD BLONDIES

PREP: 20 minutes, plus cooling
COOK: 35–40 minutes
MAKES: 16 bars
or 24 smaller squares

1 x quantity blondie batter
(page 38)

FOR THE TOPPING:
100 g (3½ oz/scant ½ cup)
good-quality custard

50 g (2 oz) rhubarb jam

50 g (2 oz) ruby (or white)
chocolate, roughly chopped

10 g (½ oz) freeze-dried strawberries

School dinner inspired, but in the very best of ways. Here the retro union of rhubarb and custard is lifted with sharp and bright strawberries, all baked into a teatime treat.

Preheat the oven to 160°C (320°F/gas mark 4) and line a 20 x 30 cm (8 x 12 inch) tin following the instructions on page 12.

Make the blondie batter following the recipe on page 38, omitting the toppings, pouring the batter into your prepared tin and levelling out the surface in the same way.

To top the blondie, use 2 teaspoons to dot the custard over the surface, followed by the rhubarb jam, then use a toothpick to ripple them through the batter. Scatter the chopped ruby or white chocolate evenly over the top, then bake as per the recipe on page 38.

As soon as the blondie is removed from the oven, scatter over the freeze-dried strawberries, then use the back of a spoon to gently press them down into the surface. Cool and slice the blondies as per the recipe on page 38.

PISTACHIO PRALINE BLONDIES

PREP: 30 minutes, plus cooling
COOK: 35–40 minutes
MAKES: 16 bars
or 24 smaller squares

1 x quantity blondie batter
(page 38)

100 g (3½ oz) pistachio paste

FOR THE PRALINE:

50 g (2 oz) pistachio slivers

100 g (3½ oz/generous ½ cup)
caster (superfine) sugar

I could eat pistachio paste with a spoon straight from the jar until the end of time. I don't, however, because it is far better showcased in this recipe, which sees it swirled through blondie batter and topped with praline.

Preheat the oven to 160°C (320°F/gas mark 4) and grease and line a 20 x 30 cm (8 x 12 inch) tin following the instructions on page 12.

To make the praline, spread the pistachio slivers over a piece of baking parchment in an even layer. Put the caster (superfine) sugar in a small pan and set over a medium heat. Leave the sugar to melt, stirring as little as possible – you can shake the pan lightly to move the sugar around if needed. Leave the caramel to cook until it is a deep caramel colour, then remove from the heat and pour directly over the pistachios. Leave the caramel to cool and set firm, then smash into shards with the end of a rolling pin.

Make the blondie batter following the recipe on page 38, omitting the toppings, pouring the batter into your prepared tin and levelling out the surface in the same way.

To top the blondie, use 2 teaspoons to dot the pistachio paste over the surface, then use a toothpick to ripple it through the batter. Scatter the pistachio praline over the top in an even layer, then bake, cool and slice the blondies as per the recipe on page 38.

PASSIONFRUIT + COCONUT BLONDIES

PREP: 20 minutes, plus making the passionfruit curd and cooling
COOK: 35–40 minutes
MAKES: 16 bars
or 24 smaller squares

1 x quantity blondie batter
(page 38)

FOR THE TOPPING:
75 g (2½ oz) passionfruit curd
(page 140)
75 g (2½ oz/generous ¼ cup) tinned coconut cream (not from a block)
50 g (2 oz) white chocolate, roughly chopped
10 g (½ oz) desiccated (dried shredded) coconut

Rich with yolky passionfruit curd and thick coconut cream, these blondies make the sunniest afternoon treat.

Preheat the oven to 160°C (320°F/gas mark 4) and line a 20 x 30 cm (8 x 12 inch) tin following the instructions on page 12.

Make the blondie batter following the recipe on page 38, omitting the toppings, and pouring the batter into your prepared tin and levelling out the surface in the same way.

To top the blondie, use 2 teaspoons to dot the passionfruit curd over the surface, followed by the coconut cream, then use a toothpick to ripple them through the batter. Scatter the chopped white chocolate and desiccated (dried shredded) coconut evenly over the top, then bake, cool and slice as per the recipe on page 38.

EGGNOG BLONDIES

PREP: 20 minutes, plus cooling
COOK: 35–40 minutes
MAKES: 16 bars
or 24 smaller square

1 x quantity blondie batter
(page 38)
1 tsp ground ginger
1 tsp ground cinnamon
½ tsp ground nutmeg
¼ tsp ground cloves

Eggnog is a festive favourite in my house. When translating my recipe into blondie form, I found that the results were better when I omitted the brandy, which, while sensible, was something I did with more than a dash of regret.

Preheat the oven to 160°C (320°F/gas mark 4) and line a 20 x 30 cm (8 x 12 inch) tin following the instructions on page 12.

Make the blondie batter following the recipe on page 38, omitting the toppings, and adding all of the ground spices at the same time as the flour, then pouring the batter into your prepared tin and levelling out the surface in the same way. Bake, cool and slice as per the recipe on page 38.

BARS
+
SLABS

BARS + SLABS

Dark Chocolate Ganache +
Almond Butter Cookie Slab

Honeycomb + Milk Chocolate Biscuit Cake

Pistachio + Blackberry Bakewell Slices

Roast Plum + Earl Grey Flapjacks

White Chocolate, Ginger +
Sour Cherry Biscuit Cake

Strawberry + Brown Sugar
Shortbread Bars

Millionaire's Diamond Shortbread

Florentine Bars

THIS CHAPTER IS A BUSY ONE. IT'S ALSO HIGHLY INDULGENT.

There's an utterly delicious almond butter and ganache cookie slab which just cries out to be warmed up and topped with ice cream. There's also biscuit cakes, sugary shortbreads topped with caramel and soft-set jam, wafer-thin Florentine bars and a simple, sticky plum flapjack which is comfort realised to me. These are confident slabs that are made to be shared – whether that's straight from the box or sitting round a table, spoons in hand.

DARK CHOCOLATE GANACHE + ALMOND BUTTER COOKIE SLAB

PREP: 20 minutes
COOK: 30 minutes
MAKES: 16 bars

FOR THE GANACHE:
100 g (3½ oz/scant ½ cup) double (heavy) cream

100 g (3½ oz) dark chocolate (minimum 70% cocoa solids), finely chopped

FOR THE COOKIE DOUGH:
100 g (3½ oz/scant ½ cup) caster (superfine) sugar

175 g (6 oz/scant 1 cup) light brown soft sugar

140 g (4½ oz) unsalted butter, soft

2 tsp vanilla bean paste

1 egg

50 g (2 oz) smooth almond butter

210 g (7½ oz/scant 1¾ cups) plain (all-purpose) flour

¼ tsp bicarbonate of soda (baking soda)

1 tsp fine sea salt

flaky sea salt, for sprinkling

NOTES

SHELF LIFE: Wrapped in airtight packaging, this will keep well for 10 days.

SUBSTITUTIONS: Swap the almond butter for runny peanut butter or tahini.

HOW TO POST: Wrap tightly in cellophane and tissue paper. Send on its own or at the bottom of a mixed box.

This slab deserves to be served in the centre of the table with spoons to dig in straight from the tin, topped with scoops of good vanilla ice cream. If you're making it to post, make sure to include a note recommending that the recipient puts it in the oven for 5–10 minutes at 180°C (350°F/gas mark 6) to reheat it just enough to bring it back to perfect warm, oozy gooeyness.

The ganache may seem like an unnecessary hassle, but is completely worth the effort. The ganache and cookie dough melt together while baking which ensures that each bite is the perfect blend of rich, slightly bitter chocolate offset by the sweet caramel of the cookie base.

Preheat the oven to 180°C (350°F/gas mark 6) and line a 20 x 30 cm (8 x 12 inch) tin following the instructions on page 12.

To make the ganache, put the cream in a small pan over a medium-low heat and heat until just starting to bubble and steam. Put the chopped chocolate in a bowl, and pour the cream directly over the top. Leave for 5 minutes without stirring, then stir the mixture a couple of times until it comes together into a smooth ganache. If you overmix the ganache and it starts to split, add teaspoons of milk one at a time, stirring between each addition, until the ganache comes back together and is smooth and glossy. Put the ganache in the fridge to firm up whilst you make the cookie dough.

To make the cookie dough, put the caster sugar, light brown soft sugar, butter and vanilla bean paste in a large mixing bowl or the bowl of a stand mixer. Beat the mixture until soft and creamy. Crack the egg into the bowl and beat until incorporated, then add the almond butter and beat again until smooth and well combined.

In a separate bowl, mix together the flour, bicarbonate of soda and fine sea salt, then tip the flour mixture into the bowl with the butter, egg and sugar mixture and mix again until you have a soft, smooth cookie dough.

Tip the cookie dough into your prepared tin and use your fingers to press it into a smooth, even layer, ensuring that the dough fills the tin right to the corners. Remove the ganache from the fridge and use 2 teaspoons to dot the ganache over the surface of the cookie dough.

Transfer to the oven to bake for 30 minutes, until puffed and golden. If you are making this to enjoy at home, simply dig in straight from the tin! If you are making this to post, leave the cookie to cool to room temperature (don't worry if it sinks a little), then remove from the tin and slice into bars.

HONEYCOMB + MILK CHOCOLATE BISCUIT CAKE

PREP: 15 minutes, plus cooling
COOK: 5 minutes
MAKES: 16 bars or 32 small squares

250 g (9 oz) unsalted butter, cubed

90 g (3¼ oz/generous ⅓ cup) caster (superfine) sugar

20 g (¾ oz) cocoa (unsweetened chocolate) powder

40 g (1½ oz) golden (light corn) syrup

½ tsp fine sea salt

450 g (1 lb) chocolate digestive biscuits (graham crackers)

100 g (3½ oz) honeycomb (my recipe is on page 149), or honeycomb chocolate bars, roughly chopped

400 g (14 oz) milk chocolate, broken into small pieces

edible gold leaf (optional)

NOTES

SHELF LIFE: Wrapped in airtight packaging, this will keep well for two weeks.

SUBSTITUTIONS: Swap the honeycomb for marshmallows, dried fruit or other chopped-up chocolate bars.

HOW TO POST: Wrap tightly in cellophane and tissue paper. This is sturdy and can be sent on its own, or at the bottom of a mixed box. It is best refrigerated on arrival if sent in the warmer months.

This throw-it-together recipe is really more of an assembly job than anything else, which makes it perfect for those times when you want something sweet but the idea of turning on the oven feels overwhelming.

I can trace the inspiration for this recipe back to my primary school days, where a similar offering called Chocolate Crunch sent me and my classmates into a sugar-fuelled frenzy! It also has roots in my childhood trips to New Zealand to see my paternal granny, Pam. Having left North London for her native Auckland in her retirement, she was a champion croquet player in the over-80s category (irrelevant but, I think, awe-inspiring), a brilliant baker and an avid endorser of Hokey Pokey, the honeycomb-studded ice cream which is something of a Kiwi national treasure. I think she would have liked my reimagining.

Line a 20 x 30 cm (8 x 12 inch) tin following the instructions on page 12.

Put the butter in a large saucepan followed by the caster sugar, cocoa powder, golden syrup and salt. Place the pan over a low heat and leave for 5 minutes, without stirring, until the butter has completely melted and enveloped the other ingredients. After 5 minutes, give the mixture a stir with a whisk to bring everything together, remove from the heat and set aside.

Put the chocolate digestive biscuits in a large mixing bowl and crush with the end of a rolling pin – I like to leave some chunkier pieces to ensure the biscuit cake has texture. Add the melted butter and cocoa mixture to the bowl and stir through the biscuits, then add most of the chopped honeycomb and stir again to ensure all the elements are well distributed. Pour the mixture into your prepared tin and level out in an even layer, ensuring the mixture fills right to the corners of the tin. Transfer to the fridge to cool and set for 2 hours.

When the cake is set, bring a pan of water to a gentle simmer and set a snug-fitting heatproof bowl over the top, ensuring that the water in the pan doesn't touch the base of the bowl. Add the chocolate to the bowl and heat until melted, stirring occasionally. Pour the melted chocolate over the cake and use a palette knife to smooth out in an even layer. Scatter the reserved honeycomb over the top, then return the cake to the fridge for 30 minutes to allow the chocolate to set.

Once the cake is set, press the sheets of gold leaf directly into the surface, if using, then use a sharp knife to slice the cake into bars.

PISTACHIO + BLACKBERRY BAKEWELL SLICES

PREP: 30 minutes, plus chilling
COOK: 45 minutes
MAKES: 16 bars

FOR THE PASTRY:

250 g (9 oz/2 cups) plain
(all-purpose) flour

½ tsp fine sea salt

125 g (4 oz) fridge-cold unsalted
butter, cubed

50 g (2 oz/scant ½ cup) icing
(confectioner's) sugar

1 egg, lightly beaten

FOR THE FILLING + TOPPING:

300 g (10½ oz/scant 1 cup)
blackberry jam

juice of 1 lime

20 g (¾ oz) freeze-dried blackberries

20 g (¾ oz) pistachio slivers

FOR THE PISTACHIO FRANGIPANE:

180 g (6½ oz/1¼ cups) shelled
pistachios (or a mix of almonds
and pistachios, if you prefer)

100 g (3½ oz) unsalted butter, soft

100 g (3½ oz/scant ½ cup) caster
(superfine) sugar

3 eggs

¼ tsp fine sea salt

zest of 1 lime

Aromatic and verdant green, pistachios have always felt extravagant to me. I like to buy the big packets of pistachios available in the international aisle at the supermarket or at the more boujee of the corner shops we have on our doorstep here in North-East London. Their rich and fragrant flavour works well in place of the traditional almonds in this recipe. When sliced, the natural green frangipane pops against the inky blackberries, and I defy anyone not to be tempted to tuck into something so pretty.

To make the pastry, put the flour and sea salt in a mixing bowl. Add the butter, toss to coat, then use the tips of your fingers to rub the butter into the flour until it resembles fine breadcrumbs and there are no big chunks of butter left. Add the icing (confectioner's) sugar to the bowl and stir to combine, then add the egg and use a fork to mix through. Working as quickly as possible so that you don't overhandle the pastry, use your hands to bring the mixture together into a smooth dough. Turn the dough out onto a lightly floured work surface, form it into a roughly rectangular shape, then wrap in cling film (plastic wrap) and transfer to the fridge to firm up for an hour.

While the dough is chilling, preheat the oven to 180°C (350°F/ gas mark 6). Line a 20 x 30 cm (8 x 12 inch) tin with baking parchment so that it fits snuggly following the instructions on page 12, but do not grease it.

To prepare the frangipane, lay the nuts on a baking sheet and toast in the oven for 10–15 minutes until fragrant. (You don't want to colour them hugely here, just toast them gently to release their oils.) Set aside and leave to cool.

Once the nuts are cooled, tip them into a food processor and blitz until fine, checking every few seconds to ensure that you are not over blitzing. They need to be finely ground but not oily.

In a large mixing bowl, cream the soft butter and sugar until light, pale and fluffy, then add the eggs one at a time, beating between each addition to ensure the mixture doesn't curdle. Once all of the eggs are incorporated, add the ground nuts, salt and lime zest and beat again until well combined. Put the frangipane in the fridge to chill until you need it.

Once the pastry has chilled, remove the prepared baking parchment from your tin and lay it flat on your work surface. Place the pastry in the centre of the baking parchment, then use a rolling pin to roll the pastry to the same size as the baking parchment.

Continues overleaf

SHELF LIFE: Wrapped in airtight packaging, these will keep well for two weeks.

SUBSTITUTION: Swap the jam for any tart fruit jam – raspberry or blackcurrant would work well. You need a sour flavour to balance the sweet frangipane. You can also swap the pistachios for almonds.

HOW TO POST: Wrap the slab tightly with cellophane and tissue paper. This is quite sturdy because of the pastry, so can be posted in a mixed box or on its own in a tightly fitted box.

Carefully lift the paper into the tin – it should slot into place easily as you have the folds and cuts in place. Prick with a fork all over, then bake in the preheated oven for 15–20 minutes, until pale and baked through. Remove from the oven and reduce the temperature to 160°C (320°F/gas mark 4).

Put the jam in a small bowl and add the lime juice. Mix until well combined, then tip the jam mixture into the tin and spread out over the pastry in an even layer. Top the jam layer with the frangipane, spreading it out in an even layer to completely fill the pastry case, then return the tart to the oven to bake for 30 minutes, until golden and firm with no wobble at all.

As soon as the tart is removed from the oven, scatter with the freeze-dried blackberries and pistachio slivers, using the back of a spoon to gently push them down into the surface of the tart. Allow to cool to room temperature before removing from the tin and slicing.

ROAST PLUM + EARL GREY FLAPJACKS

PREP: 15 minutes
COOK: 1 hour 30 minutes–2 hours
MAKES: 16 bars or 24 squares

1 Earl Grey teabag

100 ml (3½ fl oz/scant ½ cup) boiling water

400 g (14 oz) plums, stoned and quartered

1 tbsp runny honey

250 g (9 oz) unsalted butter

100 g (3½ oz/generous ¼ cup) golden (light corn) syrup

120 g (4 oz/generous ½ cup) Demerara sugar

400 g (14 oz/4 cups) rolled oats

1 tsp fine sea salt

1 tsp ground ginger

NOTES

SHELF LIFE: Wrapped in airtight packaging, these will keep well for two weeks.

SUBSTITUTIONS: Swap the plums for other roasted stone fruits – peaches, cherries and apricots would all be delicious. You could also use fresh berries instead – gooseberries, raspberries and blackberries would all work well.

HOW TO POST: Wrap the slab tightly with cellophane and tissue paper. This is quite sturdy so can be posted in a mixed box, or on its own in a tightly fitted box.

I first made a version of this recipe when I was living in Chiswick, just around the corner from a beautiful old Victoria plum tree which had, over the years, spilled over the wall of the garden in which it was rooted and taken to dropping hundreds of plums onto the adjoining street every August. I was never quite sure which side of the foraging or thieving coin collecting these plums fell on, but as nobody ever seemed to take them, temptation usually got the better of me.

Few things beat a gooey, syrupy flapjack, and the addition of sharp roasted plums brings a welcome balance to the equation.

Preheat the oven to 150°C (300°F/gas mark 3½) and line a 20 x 30 cm (8 x 12 inch) tin following the instructions on page 12.

Put the teabag in a cup, pour over the boiling water and set aside to infuse for a few minutes. Arrange the plums, cut-side up, in an ovenproof dish and drizzle over the honey. Discard the teabag and pour the infused tea over the plums. Transfer to the oven for 30–40 minutes, checking occasionally and covering with foil if they start to catch, until soft and intensified in colour. Set the plums aside to cool, then strain off the liquid (it is wonderful in cocktails or sodas). Increase the oven temperature to 180°C (350°F/gas mark 6).

Melt the butter, golden syrup and Demerara sugar in a small pan over a low heat.

Put the rolled oats, sea salt and ground ginger in a large mixing bowl and stir to combine, then pour over the melted butter and sugar mixture and stir until the oats are well coated. Add the roasted plums to the mixture and stir again briefly to just combine, then tip the mixture into the prepared baking tin and use your hands to press it into an even layer.

Transfer to the oven to bake for 30–40 minutes, until golden and just set. To aid with slicing, score the surface of the flapjacks with a sharp knife while they are still hot. Leave to cool to room temperature, then remove from the tin and slice, using the score marks as a guide.

WHITE CHOCOLATE, GINGER + SOUR CHERRY BISCUIT CAKE

PREP: 20 minutes, plus chilling
COOK: 5 minutes
MAKES: 16 bars or
32 bitesized pieces

FOR THE BASE:

400 g (14 oz) white chocolate, broken into small pieces

75 g (2½ oz) stem ginger syrup (from the jar)

100 g (3½ oz) unsalted butter, cubed

½ tsp fine sea salt

250 g (9 oz) ginger biscuits (cookies)

150 g (5 oz) stem ginger, finely chopped

20 g (¾ oz) freeze-dried sour cherries

FOR THE TOPPING:

400 g (14 oz) white chocolate, broken into small pieces

small handful of freeze-dried sour cherries

NOTES

SHELF LIFE: Wrapped in airtight packaging, this will keep well for two weeks.

SUBSTITUTIONS: You can use dried sour cherries in this recipe instead of freeze-dried. Pistachios also make a nice addition.

HOW TO POST: Wrap the slab tightly in cellophane and tissue. This is quite sturdy so can be posted in a mixed box, or on its own in a well-fitted box.

This recipe took a few attempts to get right, but I knew I was finally there when I found myself having to post the results to friends to stop me standing and eating it straight from the fridge. It is very rich thanks to the industrial quantities of white chocolate, so I recommend cutting this into bitesized pieces.

Line a 20 x 30 cm (8 x 12 inch) tin following the instructions on page 12.

To make the base, bring a pan of water to a gentle simmer, then remove from the heat and set a snug-fitting heatproof bowl over the top, ensuring that the water in the pan doesn't touch the base of the bowl. Add the white chocolate, stem ginger syrup, butter and salt to the bowl and heat until melted, stirring occasionally. It is important to keep the pan off the heat as white chocolate catches easily and will go grainy if it gets too hot. If you are struggling to melt it, you can put the pan on a low heat for a few minutes and then remove it again, using just the residual heat of the water to melt everything.

Put the ginger biscuits in a large mixing bowl and crush with the end of a rolling pin – I like to leave some chunkier pieces to ensure the biscuit cake has texture. Add the chopped stem ginger to the bowl, then pour in the melted white chocolate mixture and stir well until everything is well coated. Add the freeze-dried cherries and stir again to mix through. Pour the mixture into your prepared tin and level out in an even layer, ensuring the mixture fills right to the corners of the tin. Transfer to the fridge to cool and set for 2–3 hours.

When the cake is almost set, melt the white chocolate for the topping in the same way as you did for the cake. Pour the melted chocolate over the cake and use a palette knife to smooth it out in an even layer. Lightly crush the sour cherries for the topping, then scatter them over the top of the cake. Return the cake to the fridge for 30 minutes to allow the chocolate to set, then use a sharp knife to slice the cake into bite-sized pieces.

STRAWBERRY + BROWN SUGAR SHORTBREAD BARS

PREP: 15 minutes, plus cooling
COOK: 40 minutes
MAKES: 16 bars

FOR THE SHORTBREAD:
160 g (5½ oz) unsalted butter

80 g (3 oz/scant ½ cup)
light brown soft sugar

1 tsp vanilla bean paste

zest of 2 lemons

240 g (8½ oz/scant 2 cups)
plain (all-purpose) flour

FOR THE JAM:
½ tsp salt

600 g (1 lb 5 oz) strawberries,
hulled and cut into halves

250 g (9 oz/generous 1 cup)
caster (superfine) sugar

juice of 2 lemons

FOR THE TOPPING:
80 g (2 oz) plain (all-purpose) flour

40 g (1½ oz) cold butter

20 g (¾ oz) light brown sugar

50 g (2 oz) hazelnuts,
roughly chopped (optional)

NOTES

SHELF LIFE: Wrapped in airtight packaging, this will keep well for one week.

SUBSTITUTIONS: Swap the strawberry jam for any other flavour.

HOW TO POST: Wrap the slab tightly in cellophane and tissue paper. These are happy in a mixed box or can be posted alone in a well-fitted box.

Shortbread was one of the first things I learnt to bake. While there are – as with any recipe – numerous schools of thought as to what makes the perfect shortbread, the basic recipe is one part sugar, two parts butter, three parts flour. Here I've replaced the traditional caster sugar with light brown sugar, which gives a richer flavour and slightly shorter texture that is a nice contrast to the strawberry jam. If you prefer, you can leave off the jam and crumble layer, slice up the shortbread dough and bake as individual biscuits.

Preheat the oven to 160°C (320°F/gas mark 4) and line a 20 x 30 cm (8 x 12 inch) tin following the instructions on page 12.

In the bowl of a stand mixer or a large mixing bowl with an electric whisk, cream together the butter, light brown soft sugar, vanilla bean paste and lemon zest until smooth. Add the flour and the salt to the bowl and mix again to form a crumbly dough. Tip into the prepared baking tin and use your hands to press it into an even layer, filling right to the corners of the tin. Transfer to the oven to bake for 15–20 minutes, until pale and firm, then set aside to cool.

While the shortbread is baking, make the jam by putting the strawberries, caster (superfine) sugar and lemon juice in a large pan over a medium-high heat for 10–15 minutes, stirring occasionally, until the mixture reaches 105°C (221°F) when checked with a sugar thermometer. Remove from the heat and set aside.

To make the topping, rub the flour and butter together in a small bowl until sandy. Add the sugar and hazelnuts and mix through.

Spread the jam over the shortbread base in an even layer, then scatter over the crumble mixture. Return the shortbread to the oven for another 15–20 minutes, until golden.

Set aside to cool to room temperature, then remove from the tin and slice into bars with a sharp knife.

MILLIONAIRE'S DIAMOND SHORTBREAD

PREP: 20 minutes, plus chilling
COOK: 30 minutes
MAKES: 24 diamonds

FOR THE SHORTBREAD:

80 g (3 oz/⅓ cup) caster (superfine) sugar

160 g (5½ oz) unsalted butter

240 g (8½ oz/scant 2 cups) plain (all-purpose) flour

½ tsp salt

FOR THE CARAMEL:

1 x 397g (14 oz) tin condensed milk

1 tsp vanilla bean paste

175 g (6 oz) unsalted butter

50 g (2 oz/scant ¼ cup) caster (superfine) sugar

50 g (2 oz) golden (light corn) syrup

1 tsp salt

FOR THE TOPPING:

150 g (5 oz) milk or dark chocolate (minimum 70% cocoa solids), broken into small pieces

edible silver leaf (optional)

NOTES

SHELF LIFE: Wrapped in airtight packaging, these will keep well for two weeks.

HOW TO POST: Wrap the slab tightly in cellophane and tissue paper. This is quite sturdy so can be posted in a mixed box, or on its own in a well-fitted box.

This recipe is a classic and always a crowd-pleaser. I like mine to have an equal ratio of caramel to biscuit because, really, we all know that the thick salty caramel gets top billing here. For an extra flourish, top with silver leaf and cut into little diamonds.

Preheat the oven to 160°C (320°F/gas mark 4) and line a 20 x 30 cm (8 x 12 inch) tin following the instructions on page 12.

To make the shortbread, put the caster sugar and butter into a large bowl or the bowl of a stand mixer and cream together until smooth. Add the flour and the salt to the bowl and mix again to form a crumbly dough, then tip the mixture into the prepared baking tin and use your hands to press the shortbread into an even layer, filling right to the corners of the tin. Transfer to the oven to bake for 15–20 minutes, until pale and firm, then set aside to cool.

While the shortbread is in the oven, make the caramel by putting all the ingredients in a large pan and setting over a medium heat, stirring occasionally until it comes to the boil. Once bubbling, leave the caramel to cook for 5 minutes, until it is really thick and has darkened in colour, then pour it into the tin directly over the shortbread, tipping the tin to ensure that it covers in an even layer and fills right to the edges. Set aside to cool to room temperature, then transfer to the fridge and leave until set.

When the caramel is almost set, bring a pan of water to a gentle simmer and set a snug-fitting heatproof bowl over the top, ensuring that the water in the pan doesn't touch the base of the bowl. Add the chocolate to the bowl and heat until melted, stirring occasionally. Pour the melted chocolate over the caramel and use a palette knife to smooth out in an even layer. Return to the fridge for 30 minutes, until the chocolate is fully set.

Once the chocolate is set, press the sheets of silver leaf directly into the surface, if using, then remove the shortbread from the tin and use a sharp knife to slice it into diamond shapes.

FLORENTINE BARS

PREP: 20 minutes, plus setting
COOK: 30 minutes
MAKES: 14 bars

75 g (2½ oz) unsalted butter

75 g (2½ oz/scant ⅓ cup)
caster (superfine) sugar

75 g (2½ oz) golden (light corn) syrup

75 g (2½ oz/scant ⅔ cup)
plain (all-purpose) flour

¼ tsp fine salt

110 g (3¾ oz/1¼ cups) flaked
(slivered) almonds

75 g (2½ oz) glacé cherries, quartered

150 g (5 oz) dark chocolate
(minimum 70% cocoa solids),
broken into small pieces

NOTES

SHELF LIFE: Wrapped in airtight
packaging, this will keep well for
two weeks.

SUBSTITUTIONS: Try swapping
the cherries for dried banana to make
banoffee Florentines. Pistachio slivers
work well in place of some or all of the
almonds, too.

HOW TO POST: Carefully stack
6–8 Florentine bars on top of each
other, then wrap tightly in cellophane
and tissue paper. These should go at
the top of a mixed box or be posted
alone in a well-fitted box.

There is something wildly cheering about glacé cherries. Despite tasting nothing like the fresh cherries they once were, they are gloriously retro and their lurid colour never fails to entice. However, they could be swapped out for candied citrus if you have better taste than me or – for full retro effect – angelica. This recipe is more than just a foil for glacé fruit – the combination of caramel, almond and dark chocolate is a beautiful one, and a stack of these is sure to lift spirits.

Preheat the oven to 175°C (345°F/gas mark 5½) and line a 20 x 30 cm (8 x 12 inch) tin following the instructions on page 12.

Put the butter, caster (superfine) sugar and golden (light corn) syrup in a large pan over a low heat, until the sugar has dissolved and the butter has melted. Increase the heat to medium and leave to cook until the mixture is foaming and just starting to darken in colour.

Add the flour and salt to the pan and, working quickly, mix with a wooden spoon until combined. Add the almonds and cherries, then mix again to combine. Pour the mixture into your prepared tin, pressing it down to form an even layer that fills right to the edges. Transfer to the oven and cook for 15–20 minutes, until deep golden and bubbling. Set aside to cool on a wire rack.

Once cooled, lay a sheet of baking parchment over the top of the Florentines, then flip upside down, remove the tin and peel away the original paper, so that the flat side of the Florentines is facing up.

Bring a pan of water to a gentle simmer and set a snug-fitting heatproof bowl over the top, ensuring that the water in the pan doesn't touch the base of the bowl. Add the chocolate to the bowl and heat until melted, stirring occasionally. Pour the melted chocolate over the Florentines and use a palette knife to smooth it out in an even layer. Leave to partially set for around 30 minutes (not in the fridge), then use a serrated knife or fork to create a wiggly pattern on the chocolate.

Once the chocolate has fully set at room temperature (not in the fridge), use a heavy knife to cut the slab into bars or triangles.

CAKES

CAKES

Apple + Blackberry Crumble Cake

Vegan Dark Chocolate + Coconut Cake

Fig, Ginger + Black Cherry Christmas Cake

Gin + Lemon Drizzle Cake

Hazelnut Cake

Sour Cream + Blueberry Cake

Summer Stone Fruit Friand Cake

Banana Breakfast Cake

Sticky Stem Ginger Cake

Lemon + Rose Battenbergs

I TRY NOT TO HAVE FAVOURITES, BUT SOMETIMES ONLY CAKE WILL DO.

Perfect for teatime but also for
breakfast, elevenses or simply
a sugar boost whenever it is needed,
the recipes that follow are not intricate
or elaborate. They are simple-to-
assemble, flavour-led cakes which
make the most of what's in season
and celebrate the things that –
I think – people really want to eat.

APPLE + BLACKBERRY CRUMBLE CAKE

PREP: 25 minutes, plus cooling
COOK: 40–50 minutes
MAKES: 16 cake bars

175 g (6 oz) unsalted butter, cubed

175 g (6 oz/scant 1 cup)
light brown soft sugar

3 eggs

100 g (3½ oz/generous ¾ cup)
self-raising (self-rising) flour

75 g (2½ oz/scant ¾ cup)
ground almonds

½ tsp baking powder

½ tsp salt

150 g (5 oz/scant ½ cup)
blackberry jam

200 g (7 oz) Bramley or
sharp eating apple, such as
Granny Smith, peeled and cored

FOR THE CRUMBLE:
60 g (2 oz/½ cup) plain
(all-purpose) flour

30 g (1 oz) unsalted butter

20 g (¾ oz) Demerara sugar

NOTES

SHELF LIFE: This is best eaten
within five days of baking, so should
be posted out using next-day
postal services.

SUBSTITUTIONS: Try swapping
the apple for thin slices of pear, and
use any jam you have to hand.

HOW TO POST: Wrap a small slab
tightly in cellophane, followed by
tissue paper. Do not stack the slices.
These are best sent on their own in
a snug-fitting box.

Apple desserts are among my very favourites – I love them baked with dried fruit, nuts and spices, encased in a thick pie crust and, of course, sharp and soft against a sweet crumble topping. Which is lucky, perhaps, given the vast quantities of knobbly cookers that my grandparents pick every autumn from the little orchard my grandad planted decades ago on their farm in Lincolnshire.

The brown sugar and nutty base of this cake reminds me of all of my favourite apple desserts, and perhaps that's why I love it so much. Slice the apples finely to ensure they don't sink when baking. Don't be tempted to soak them in water to stop them browning, either – just work quickly and get it in the oven as soon as the crumble is on.

Preheat the oven to 170°C (340°F/gas mark 5) and line a 20 x 30 cm (8 x 12 inch) tin following the instructions on page 12.

In the bowl of a stand mixer with the paddle attachment or a large mixing bowl with an electric whisk, cream the butter and light brown soft sugar until pale and fluffy, then crack the eggs into the bowl one at a time, beating well between each addition.

Add the flour, ground almonds, baking powder and salt to the bowl and mix until just combined, then transfer the mixture to the prepared tin and use a palette knife to spread it out in an even layer.

Using 2 teaspoons, dot the blackberry jam over the surface of the cake, then use a palette knife to ripple it through the batter.

Using a sharp knife, slice the apples as finely as you can, then, working quickly so that the apple doesn't start to brown, lay the slices over the surface of the cake in a decorative pattern, ensuring that the whole cake is covered in an even layer.

To make the crumble topping, put the flour and butter in a bowl and rub together with your fingers until the mixture resembles fine breadcrumbs. Stir the Demerera sugar through the crumble, then scatter it evenly over the surface of the cake.

Transfer to the oven to bake for 40–50 minutes, until golden, well risen and a skewer inserted into the centre comes out clean. Set aside to cool to room temperature, then remove from the tin and slice with a sharp knife.

VEGAN DARK CHOCOLATE + COCONUT CAKE

PREP: 15 minutes, plus cooling
COOK: 25–30 minutes
MAKES: 16 cake bars

100 g (3½ oz) coconut oil, melted

175 g (6 oz/scant ¾ cup) plant-based coconut yoghurt

200 g (7 oz/generous ¾ cup) plant-based milk, such as soy or coconut

1 tbsp apple cider vinegar

250 g (9 oz/generous 1 cup) caster (superfine) or coconut sugar

175 g (6 oz/scant 1½ cups) plain (all-purpose) flour

80 g (3 oz/scant ⅔ cup) cocoa (unsweetened chocolate) powder

½ tsp fine salt

1 tsp baking powder

1 tsp bicarbonate of soda (baking soda)

150 g (5 oz) vegan dark chocolate, finely chopped

30 g (1 oz) coconut chips or desiccated (dried shredded) coconut

flaky sea salt, to finish

NOTES

SHELF LIFE: This cake will keep well for up to a week when wrapped tightly or stored in an airtight container.

SUBSTITUTIONS: If you don't wish to make a vegan cake, the plant-based dairy substitutes can be swapped for dairy equivalents.

HOW TO POST: Wrap a small slab of slices tightly in cellophane, followed by tissue paper. Do not stack the slices. These are best sent on their own in a snug-fitting box.

I developed this recipe a couple of years ago when I was first tasked with making a vegan wedding cake. I experimented with avocados, and while I know a lot of bakers do wonders with them in plant-based cakes, I found that a careful blend of oil, vegan yoghurt and milk was the best way of achieving a stable, moist and delicious crumb. Rich with creamy coconut and slathered with a thick slick of dark chocolate, this is a moreish and indulgent cake, and is at its best a couple of days after baking, which makes it perfect for posting.

Preheat the oven to 160°C (320°F/gas mark 4) and line a 20 x 30 cm (8 x 12 inch) tin following the instructions on page 12.

Put the melted coconut oil, coconut yoghurt, plant-based milk and apple cider vinegar in a bowl and whisk to combine.

In a separate bowl, combine the caster or coconut sugar, flour, cocoa powder, salt, baking powder and bicarbonate of soda, then pour the yoghurt and milk mixture into the bowl with the dry ingredients and whisk until smooth and well combined.

Pour the cake batter into the prepared tin and use a palette knife to smooth the surface in an even layer. Transfer to the oven and bake for 25–30 minutes, until risen and a skewer inserted into the centre comes out clean. Set aside to cool.

While the cake is cooling, bring a pan of water to a gentle simmer and set a snug-fitting heatproof bowl over the top, ensuring that the water in the pan doesn't touch the base of the bowl. Add the chocolate to the bowl and heat until melted, stirring occasionally. Pour the melted chocolate over the cooled cake and use a palette knife to smooth it out in an even layer. Sprinkle over the coconut chips or desiccated coconut, or a good sprinkling of flaky sea salt, and leave to cool until the chocolate fully sets before slicing.

FIG, GINGER + BLACK CHERRY CHRISTMAS CAKE

PREP: 30 minutes,
plus soaking and maturing
COOK: 1 hour +
MAKES: 16 cake bars

150 g (5 oz) dried figs, chopped
into 1 cm (½ inch) cubed pieces

250 g (8 oz) sultanas (golden raisins),
raisins or currants (or a mix)

100 g (3½ oz) black glacé
cherries, halved

75 g (2½ oz) glacé ginger,
finely chopped

75 g (2½ oz) candied citrus peel,
finely chopped

100 g (3½ oz) dried apricots,
chopped into 1 cm (½ inch)
cubed pieces

100 ml (3½ fl oz/½ cup) rum, brandy
or sloe gin, plus extra for feeding

150 g (5 oz) unsalted butter, cubed

90 g (3¼ oz/scant ½ cup) dark
brown soft sugar

2 eggs

1 lemon

1 orange

1 tbsp treacle

½ tbsp tamarind paste

125 g (4 oz/1 cup) self-raising
(self-rising) flour

75 g (2½ oz/generous ⅔ cup)
ground almonds

½ tsp ground ginger

1 tsp ground mixed spice

½ tsp salt

50 g (2 oz/⅓ cup) blanched almonds,
finely chopped

25 g (1 oz/scant ¼ cup) shelled
pistachios, finely chopped

75 g (2½ oz/scant ¼ cup) apricot jam

500 g (1 lb 2 oz) marzipan

500 g (1 lb 2 oz) white fondant icing, or
1 x quantity of Royal Icing (page 149)

The 5th of November is Bonfire Night in the UK, but it's also the date of another tradition in my family – the day that we start making our Christmas cakes. The date was chosen on purpose so that we always remember (remember) to start the cakes early, but there's something rather festive about making this familiar recipe to the gentle chorus of fireworks.

The cake starts life with slow-soaked, liqueur-rich fruit, before being enriched with citrus, festive spices and treacle. Once baked, the cake is fed with more booze in the run-up to Christmas, resulting in the softest, most decadent crumb on the big day. In my parent's house, the Christmas cake is cut in mid-December to give us a bit of a head start (it used to still be around well into the spring).

If you are going to the effort of making Christmas cake, I strongly recommend doubling the below recipe and making two tins. Slabs of this make great gifts.

My recipe replaces some of the traditional currant bulk with chopped dried figs, apricots, cherries and ginger, which I think results in better flavour and texture. The addition of tamarind was something I first came across in Fiona Cairn's recipe, and brings a sour note that is utterly inspired.

The night before you plan to bake the cake, weigh the figs, sultanas, glacé cherries, glacé ginger, candied citrus peel, zest of the orange, zest of the lemon and dried apricots into a heavy-based saucepan. Drench with the rum, brandy or sloe gin, and the juice of the orange and lemon, then set over a gentle heat. Slowly bring to a simmer, then remove from the heat as soon as the liquid starts to bubble. Cover and leave to steep overnight.

The following day, preheat the oven to 160°C (320°F/gas mark 4) and line a 20 x 30 cm (8 x 12 inch) tin following the instructions on page 12.

In the bowl of a stand mixer with the paddle attachment or a large bowl with an electric whisk, cream the butter and dark brown soft sugar until light and fluffy, then add the eggs, treacle and tamarind and mix again at a low speed to just combine.

Add the flour, ground almonds, ground ginger, mixed spice and salt and fold through the mixture, then add the chopped nuts and the soaked fruit (liquid and all) and stir again until just combined.

Continues overleaf

NOTES

SHELF LIFE: The cake will keep for months – we've been known to still be eating our Christmas cake at Easter! But once iced, it's best eaten within two weeks.

SUBSTITUTIONS: There are so many! You can switch up the dried fruits and nuts as you please (just be sure to stick to the same total quantities), and you could of course ice the cake with Royal Icing (find my recipe on page 149) if you prefer a textured finish. I've also fed mine with sloe gin instead of brandy in past years.

HOW TO POST: Wrap a slab tightly in cellophane, followed by tissue paper. Do not stack the slices on top of each other. This can be either be sent at the bottom of a mixed box, or on its own in a snug-fitting box. Be warned – this cake is heavy!

Pour the mixture into your prepared tin and use a palette knife to smooth the surface in an even layer. Transfer to the oven for 1 hour then check if it is ready by inserting a skewer into the centre to see if it comes out clean. If not, return the cake to the oven for 15 minutes, then check again. If the cake starts to brown too much during cooking, place a sheet of foil over the top to protect the surface.

Once baked, set the cake aside to cool in the tin for 30 minutes, then turn it out and leave to cool to room temperature. Once cooled, wrap the cake in a layer of baking parchment followed by a layer of foil, then set it aside in a cool, dark corner of your kitchen for up to 2 months. Once a week, unwrap the cake and brush the surface with a teaspoon or so of brandy, then wrap the cake again and return it to its corner.

Two days before you plan to serve or send the cake, warm the apricot jam until loose and brush over the surface of the cake. Knead the marzipan a little to soften it, then use a rolling pin to roll it into a rectangle roughly the size of the cake. Carefully lift the marzipan onto the cake, then trim the edges to neaten. (I like to only cover the top of mine and leave the sides bare, but you could also cover the sides, if you prefer.) Set the marzipan-covered cake aside to allow the marzipan to firm up overnight.

The next day, if you are using fondant icing, brush the marzipan with a little brandy, then roll out the fondant icing to roughly the same size as the cake. Carefully lift the icing over the marzipan, smoothing it down neatly, then trim the edges. If using Royal Icing, dollop on top of the cake and use a palette knife to spread and swoop. Allow to harden for 3–4 hours before slicing, but be sure to slice before it sets fully.

GIN + LEMON DRIZZLE CAKE

PREP: 20 minutes, plus cooling
and making the lemon curd
COOK: 40 minutes
MAKES: 16 cake bars

FOR THE CAKE:
4 eggs, weighed in their shells
Equal weights of:
unsalted butter
caster (superfine) sugar
self-raising (self-rising) flour
2 tbsp milk
½ tsp salt
1 lemon
150 g (5 oz) lemon curd (page 140)

FOR THE SYRUP:
100 g (3½ oz/generous ⅔ cup)
caster (superfine) sugar
juice of the lemon
75 ml (2½ fl oz) gin

FOR THE TOPPING:
100 g (3½ oz/generous ⅔ cup)
caster (superfine) sugar
2–3 tsp gin

NOTES

SHELF LIFE: This cake should
be eaten with 2–3 days of baking,
so is best sent using next-day
postal services.

SUBSTITUTIONS: Try swapping
the lemon zest, juice and curd
for lime or grapefruit instead.

HOW TO POST: Wrap a small
slab of slices tightly in cellophane,
followed by tissue paper. Do not
stack the slices on top of each other.
These are best sent on their own
in a snug-fitting box.

*This recipe is a reworking of my recipe for gin and tonic loaf cake,
which I first shared on my baking blog Pudding Lane back in 2014.
That recipe went viral which, really, should have been a surprise to
nobody given the mother-ruining measure of gin that goes into the
drizzle. The gin has gone nowhere, but it's been joined by an enriching
swirl of lemon curd, which brings zing and cleanses the palette –
much like a slice of citrus in your evening G&T.*

Preheat the oven to 170°C (340°F/gas mark 5) and line a 20 x 30 cm
(8 x 12 inch) tin following the instructions on page 12.

Weigh the eggs in their shells, then measure out the same
weight each of unsalted butter, caster sugar and self-raising flour.

In the bowl of a stand mixer with the paddle attachment or a
large mixing bowl with an electric whisk, cream the butter and caster
sugar until pale and fluffy. Add the milk to the bowl, then crack the
eggs in one at a time, beating well between each addition. Add the
flour, salt and zest of the lemon to the bowl and mix again until
just combined.

Pour the mixture into the prepared tin, using a palette knife to
smooth out the surface in an even layer. Using 2 teaspoons, dot the
lemon curd over the surface of the cake, then use a toothpick to ripple
it through the batter.

Transfer the cake to the oven to bake for 25–30 minutes,
until golden and risen, and a skewer inserted into the centre comes
out clean. Set aside to cool.

While the cake is cooling, make the syrup by putting the caster
sugar and lemon juice in a small pan over a low heat, until the sugar
has dissolved, then turn up the heat to medium and leave to bubble
until reduced by half. Add the gin to the pan and leave to cook for
a couple more minutes, until thick and syrupy. Brush the hot syrup
generously over the cake in the tin.

To make the topping, put the caster sugar in a small bowl and
add enough gin to make a sugary paste. Spread this mixture over the
cake, then set aside to harden into a crunchy crust before removing
from the tin and slicing.

HAZELNUT CAKE

PREP: 30–40 minutes, plus cooling
COOK: 1 hour 35 minutes
MAKES: 16 cake bars

FOR THE CAKE:

150 g (5 oz/generous 1 cup) hazelnuts

225 g (8 oz) unsalted butter,
at room temperature

225 g (8 oz/scant 1 cup)
caster (superfine) sugar

4 eggs

100 g (3½ oz/generous ¾ cup)
gluten-free flour

1 tsp baking powder

½ tsp salt

FOR THE TOPPING:

50 g (2 oz/scant ⅓ cup) hazelnuts

75 g (2½ oz/⅓ cup) caster
(superfine) sugar

200 g (7 oz) golden icing sugar

NOTES

SHELF LIFE: This should be eaten
within four days of baking, so is best
sent using next-day postal services.

HOW TO POST: Wrap a small
slab of slices tightly in cellophane,
followed by tissue paper. Ensure the
topping has set fully before wrapping.
Do not stack the slices. These are best
sent on their own in a snug-fitting box.

This cake is a riff on one of my most popular gluten-free wedding cakes. Ground hazelnuts bring a delicious moist texture which is often missing in gluten-free cakes, and this also keeps well which makes it perfect for posting. I like to finish this cake with a simple golden icing sugar glaze and a sprinkling of hazelnut praline, but it is delicious without adornment if you prefer to keep things simple.

Preheat the oven to 170°C (340°F/gas mark 5) and line a 20 x 30 cm (8 x 12 inch) tin following the instructions on page 12.

Spread the hazelnuts out on a baking sheet and toast in the oven for 10–15 minutes, until golden and fragrant. Set aside until cool enough to handle, then roughly chop 25 g (1 oz) of the nuts and set aside. Put the remaining 125 g (4 oz) into the bowl of a food processor and blitz to coarse powder. Set aside.

In the bowl of a stand mixer with the paddle attachment or a large mixing bowl with an electric whisk, cream the butter and caster sugar until pale and fluffy, then crack the eggs into the bowl one at a time, beating well between each addition. Add the flour, blitzed hazelnuts, baking powder and salt and mix again until just combined.

Pour the mixture into the prepared tin, using a palette knife to smooth out the surface in an even layer. Transfer the cake to the oven to bake for 25–35 minutes, until golden and risen, and a skewer inserted into the centre comes out clean. Set aside to cool.

While the cake is cooling, make the topping. To make the praline, spread the reserved chopped hazelnuts over a piece of baking parchment. Place the caster sugar in a small pan and set over a medium heat. Allow the sugar to melt, stirring as little as possible – you can shake the pan lightly to move the sugar around if you need to. Allow it to cook until it is a deep caramel colour, then remove from the heat and pour over the hazelnuts. Allow to cool, then smash up using the end of a rolling pin.

Combine the icing sugar with enough water to make a thick paste, then pour over the cake and tilt it to encourage it into the corners. Top with the hazelnut praline.

SOUR CREAM + BLUEBERRY CAKE

PREP: 20 minutes, plus cooling
COOK: 20–25 minutes
MAKES: 16 cake bars

2 eggs

225 g (8 oz/scant 1 cup) caster (superfine) sugar

225 g (8 oz/scant 1 cup) sour cream or plain yoghurt

zest and juice of 1 lemon

100 g (3½ oz/1 cup) ground almonds

150 g (5 oz/scant 1¼ cups) self-raising (self-rising) flour

1 tsp baking powder

½ tsp salt

100 g (3½ oz/⅔ cup) blueberries or other berries

200 g (7 oz/generous 1½ cups) icing (confectioner's) sugar

NOTES

SHELF LIFE: This should be eaten within four days of baking, so is best sent using next-day postal services.

SUBSTITUTIONS: Swap the blueberries for raspberries, blackberries, roasted plums, apricots or rhubarb.

HOW TO POST: Wrap a small slab of slices tightly in cellophane, followed by tissue paper. Ensure the glaze has set fully before wrapping. Do not stack the slices. These are best sent on their own in a snug-fitting box.

I love the texture of this cake. The sour cream brings a slight chewiness to the crumb and a tang of flavour which I find incredibly hard to resist, and often one slice of this quickly leads to a second! This cake is also delicious when baked as a loaf cake, for which you can follow the quantities below to fill a large loaf tin – you will just need to increase the baking time to 35–40 minutes.

Preheat the oven to 170°C (340°F/gas mark 5) and line a 20 x 30 cm (8 x 12 inch) tin following the instructions on page 12.

Crack the eggs into a mixing bowl with the sugar, then whisk for 4–5 minutes until the mixture is pale, airy and forms ribbons when you drag the whisk across the surface. Add the sour cream and lemon zest, and gently fold into the mixture. Sieve in the almonds, flour, baking powder and salt, and fold until the mixture is combined. (Discard any larger pieces of almond or almond skin that are left in the sieve.) Add the blueberries and gently mix through.

Pour the mixture into the prepared tin, using a palette knife to smooth out the surface in an even layer. Transfer the cake to the oven to bake for 20–25 minutes, until golden and risen, and a skewer inserted into the centre comes out clean. Set aside to cool on a wire rack.

While the cake is cooling, whisk the icing sugar with the lemon juice to make a smooth glaze. Pour over the cake in an even layer, then leave to set before removing from the tin and slicing.

SUMMER STONE FRUIT FRIAND CAKE

PREP: 15 minutes, plus chilling and making the salted caramel
COOK: 1 hour 15 minutes
MAKES: 16 bars
or 24 smaller squares

FOR THE ROASTED FRUIT:
600 g stone fruit (a combination of apricots, cherries, peaches, plums and nectarines works well)

1 lemon

50 g (2 oz/scant ¼ cup) caster (superfine) sugar

2 tsp vanilla bean paste

FOR THE CAKE:
200 g (7 oz) unsalted butter, cubed

250 g (9 oz) egg white (about 6–7 eggs)

175 g (6 oz/scant 1½ cups) icing (confectioner's) sugar

50 g (2 oz/scant ½ cup) plain (all-purpose) flour

175 g (6 oz/scant 1¾ cups) ground almonds

½ tsp fine sea salt

150 g (5 oz/scant ½ cup) stone fruit jam

zest of the lemon

NOTES

SHELF LIFE: This should be eaten within five days of baking, so is best sent using next-day postal services.

SUBSTITUTIONS: Swap the fruit for roasted strawberries or figs, depending on the season.

HOW TO POST: Wrap a small slab tightly in cellophane, followed by tissue paper. These are best sent on their own in a snug-fitting box.

This cake uses a friand batter, a deliberate commitment to translating my favourite little cakes into postal, shareable form. The sponge is so nutty and soft that this cake is perfect for dessert, or even as part of a breakfast spread. Cake for breakfast is commonplace in many European countries, and who am I to question such wonderful logic?

Roasting the fruit until they are caramelised and jammy removes much of the excess moisture, ensuring that the sponge encasing them travels intact when posted.

Preheat the oven to 180°C (350°F/gas mark 6) and line a 20 x 30 cm (8 x 12 inch) tin following the instructions on page 12.

Chop your chosen fruits in half and remove any stones, then slice the flesh into evenly sized pieces. Put the fruit in the tin and pour over the juice of the lemon, then add the caster sugar and vanilla bean paste. Transfer to the oven to bake for 45–55 minutes, until the fruit is soft and shrivelled, but still holding its shape. Transfer to a bowl and set aside to cool completely before using.

Wash up the tin, then reline it with baking parchment. Lower the oven temperature to 170°C (340°F/gas mark 5).

To make the cake, melt the butter in a small pan over a low heat, then turn up the heat to medium-high and leave to bubble and foam for about 5 minutes, until the milk solids turn golden brown. Remove from the heat and set aside to cool slightly while you prepare the other ingredients.

Put the egg whites in the bowl of a stand mixer with the whisk attached or in a large mixing bowl with an electric whisk, and whisk for a couple of minutes to form soft, foamy peaks (you are not looking for stiff meringue-like peaks here).

In a separate bowl, sift together the icing sugar, flour, ground almonds and salt. (Discard any larger pieces of almond or almond skin that are left in the sieve.) Add the lemon zest to the bowl, then tip this mixture into the bowl with the whisked egg whites and use a metal spoon to gently fold the flour mixture through the meringue. Be careful not to overmix and take the volume out of the egg whites at this stage, as this will result in a flat cake. Once combined, pour the browned butter into the bowl and fold through again until just combined.

Pour the cake batter into the prepared tin, then use 2 teaspoons to dot the jam over the surface of the batter. Dot the roasted fruit over the surface of the cake, then transfer to the oven to bake for 30–35 minutes, until golden, well risen and an inserted skewer comes out clean. Leave to cool to room temperature before removing from the tin and slicing.

BANANA BREAKFAST CAKE

PREP: 20 minutes plus cooling
COOK: 30–40 minutes
MAKES: 16 cake bars

400 g (14 oz/4 cups) rolled oats

4 eggs

200 g (7 oz/generous ¾ cup)
plain yoghurt

100 g (3½ oz) coconut
or light brown sugar

1 tsp vanilla bean paste

75 g (2½ oz) coconut oil, melted

4 ripe bananas, mashed with a fork

2 tsp baking powder

½ tsp fine salt

1 tsp ground cinnamon

150 g (5 oz) dates, stoned
and roughly chopped

20 g (¾ oz) coconut chips (optional)

NOTES

SHELF LIFE: This will keep well
for up to a week when wrapped tightly
or stored in an airtight container.

SUBSTITUTIONS: Swap the oat
flour for wholemeal wheat, spelt
or a mixture of the three.

HOW TO POST: Wrap a slab tightly
in cellophane, followed by tissue
paper. These are best sent on their
own in a snug-fitting box.

*More cake for breakfast! Oats, bananas, eggs, yoghurt, dates –
breakfast, no? This cake was inspired by breakfast muffins, baked
porridge, Dutch babies and almost everything in between. Blitzing
oats into a flour is a great way to bring a little extra nutritional benefit,
and also creates a delicious texture to stand up to the banana.
Delicious as part of a brunch spread or on the go for breakfast in
a rush, and just as good at teatime.*

Preheat the oven to 170°C (340°F/gas mark 5) and line a 20 x 30 cm
(8 x 12 inch) tin following the instructions on page 12.

Set 20g (¾ oz) of the oats aside for later and put the remaining
oats in the bowl of a food processor and blitz to a powdery, flour-like
consistency.

In the bowl of a stand mixer with the whisk attachment or a large
mixing bowl with an electric whisk, whisk the eggs, yoghurt, sugar and
vanilla paste until well combined. Add the coconut oil and mashed
banana to the bowl and mix again briefly to combine.

In a separate bowl, combine the blitzed oats, baking powder,
salt and ground cinnamon. Add this mixture to the bowl with the wet
ingredients along with two-thirds of the chopped dates, and mix again
until everything is well combined.

Pour the mixture into the prepared cake tin and level the surface
with a palette knife. Scatter the remaining chopped dates, reserved
rolled oats and coconuts chips, if using, evenly over the surface,
then transfer to the oven to bake for 30–35 minutes, until the cake is
golden, risen and a skewer inserted into the centre comes out clean.
Set aside to cool to room temperature before removing from the tin
and slicing.

STICKY
STEM GINGER CAKE

PREP: 15 minutes, plus cooling
COOK: 30–40 minutes
MAKES: 16 cake bars

225 g (8 oz/scant ⅔ cup) treacle

225 g (8 oz) unsalted butter, cubed

110 ml (3¾ oz/scant ½ cup) whole milk

150 g (5 oz/generous ¾ cup) dark muscovado sugar

225 g (8 oz/generous 1¾ cups) self-raising (self-rising) flour

1 tsp baking powder

3 tsp ground ginger

1 tsp ground mixed spice

½ tsp ground cardamom

¼ tsp ground black pepper

½ tsp salt

2 eggs

150 g (5 oz) crystallised stem ginger, finely chopped

NOTES

SHELF LIFE: This will keep well for up to a week when wrapped tightly or stored in an airtight container.

SUBSTITUTIONS: For an additional flourish, you could finish the cake with a lemon water icing

HOW TO POST: Wrap a slab tightly in cellophane, followed by tissue paper. These are best sent on their own in a snug-fitting box.

Deliciously dense with treacle, heavily spiced and rich with chunks of sweet stem ginger, this in an intrinsically wintery cake. I first tested this recipe on a particularly bleak weekend shortly after Christmas during the third lockdown here in the UK. It was one of those cold and wet weekends where the prospect of a dash to the shops was sufficiently unappealing to see me raiding the cupboards and making the most of what they yielded. The results were just the tonic to my January blues.

Preheat the oven to 180°C (350°F/gas mark 6) and line a 20 x 30 cm (8 x 12 inch) tin following the instructions on page 12.

Put the treacle, butter, milk and sugar in a pan over a low heat, stirring occasionally, until the butter has melted and the sugar has dissolved.

Meanwhile, combine the flour, baking powder, ground ginger, mixed spice, ground cardamom, black pepper and the salt in a large mixing bowl. Once the butter and treacle mixture has fully melted, pour it over the dry ingredients and whisk quickly to combine.

Crack the eggs into a small bowl and beat briefly to combine, then pour them into the bowl with the cake batter and whisk the mixture to bring everything together. Pour the mixture into the prepared baking tin and level out the surface with a palette knife.

Transfer to the oven to bake for 25 minutes, then remove and scatter the crystallised stem ginger evenly over the surface. Return to the oven and continue to cook for another 10–15 minutes, until risen and a skewer inserted into the centre comes out clean. Set aside to cool to room temperature before removing from the tin and slicing.

LEMON + ROSE BATTENBERGS

PREP: 40 minutes,
plus chilling and resting
COOK: 25 minutes
MAKES: 3 battenbergs

180 g (6¼ oz) unsalted butter,
at room temperature

180 g (6¼ oz/generous ¾ cup)
caster (superfine) sugar

3 eggs

90 g (3¼ oz/¾ cup) self-raising
(self-rising) flour

90 g (3¼ oz/scant 1 cup)
ground almonds

1 tsp baking powder

½ tsp fine salt

zest of ½ lemon

1 tsp rose water

few dabs pink gel food colouring

200 g (7 oz/scant ⅔ cup) apricot jam

750 g (1 lb 10 oz) white marzipan

NOTES

SHELF LIFE: These should
be eaten within five days of
baking, so are best sent using
next-day postal services.

SUBSTITUTIONS: Swap the
rose water for orange blossom
water, or almond essence if you
prefer a classic battenberg.

HOW TO POST: Wrap tightly
in cellophane, followed by tissue
paper. These are best sent on
their own in a snug-fitting box.

*While I love the classic almond flavour, I've added lemon and rose
to my version, which I find a pleasing pairing to the pink and yellow
sponges. The battenbergs are easier to slice and assemble the day
after baking.*

Preheat the oven to 170°C (340°F/gas mark 5) and line a 20 x 30 cm
(8 x 12 inch) tin following the instructions on page 12. Once lined, cut
a piece of foil the same width as the tin, fold it in half, then place across
the centre of the narrow axis of the tin, creating two separate sections.

Cream the butter and caster sugar until pale and fluffy, then
crack the eggs into the bowl one at a time, beating well between each
addition. Add the flour, ground almonds, baking powder and salt and
mix again until just combined.

Decant half the batter into a separate bowl. Add the lemon zest
to the first bowl and mix. Add the rose water and a small dab of pink
food colouring to the second bowl, then mix until the colour is even.

Pour each of the cake batters into a separate side of the
prepared tin, levelling the surface with a palette knife, then transfer
to the oven to bake for 20–25 minutes, until a skewer inserted into
the centre of the cake comes out clean. Set aside to cool completely.

When you are ready to assemble, trim the edges and surface
of each cake so you have 2 even, sharp-edged rectangles. Check that
both cakes are the same height, levelling off the taller one if needed.

Carefully measure the height of each cake, then cut long strips
as wide as they are high. You should end up with 6 strips of each
type of cake – enough for 3 battenbergs.

Gently warm the apricot jam. Cut the marzipan into 3 equal
pieces. Lay a large sheet of cling film (plastic wrap) on the counter
and place one of the pieces of marzipan in the centre. Roll it out to
the same length as your strips of cake.

Brush 2 strips of each colour sponge with the apricot jam on
all sides except the ends, then assemble the 4 pieces together in a
two-up, two-down chequerboard arrangement. Brush with more jam,
then place the cake in the centre of the marzipan and use the cling
film to wrap the marzipan around the 4 long sides. Trim off any excess
marzipan, then fully enclose the cake in the cling film and use your
fingers to mould the edges so they are sharp and square.

Repeat until you have 3 wrapped battenbergs, then transfer the
cakes to the fridge for a few hours to firm up. Once chilled, remove the
cling film and carefully slice the ends of each cake to neaten the edges
and display a sharp chequerboard pattern.

BISCUITS

BISCUITS

Neapolitan Sandwich Cookies

**Peanut Butter + Jam
Thumbprint Cookies**

Rosemary + Walnut Crackers

**Parmesan + Cayenne
Pepper Biscuits**

Cocoa + Macadamia Sables

Tahini + Milk Chocolate Cookies

Citrusy Pine Nut Amaretti

Rye + Apricot Biscotti

DIY Iced Vanilla Biscuit Box

DIY Gingerbread Box

FEW THINGS DELIGHT ME MORE THAN A BAG OF HOMEMADE BISCUITS, TIED WITH RIBBON AND CAREFULLY PACKED TO TRAVEL.

Whether it's biscotti for dunking, soft amaretti or savoury biscuits sent with membrillo, these are the perfect pick-me-ups to send in the post. There's also a couple of DIY ideas which allow your recipient to decorate the biscuits themselves.

NEAPOLITAN SANDWICH COOKIES

PREP: 40 minutes, plus chilling
COOK: 20 minutes
MAKES: 35–40 cookies

FOR THE COOKIES:

100 g (3½ oz) unsalted butter, soft

100 g (3½ oz/scant ½ cup) caster (superfine) sugar

¼ tsp fine sea salt

1 egg yolk

200 g (7 oz/1⅔ cups) plain (all-purpose) flour

1 tsp vanilla bean paste

1–2 tsp whole milk, as needed

20 g (¾ oz) cocoa (unsweetened chocolate) powder

FOR THE BUTTERCREAM:

40 g (1½ oz) unsalted butter, soft

125 g (4 oz/1 cup) icing (confectioner's) sugar

1–2 tsp whole milk

10 g (½ oz) freeze-dried strawberries, crushed to a powder

NOTES

GET AHEAD: Make the dough and refrigerate for a few days before baking.

SHELF LIFE: These keep well for up to a week if wrapped tightly or stored in an airtight container.

HOW TO POST: Stack in a tower and wrap in cellophane and then tissue paper.

Inspired by the vast tubs of wonderfully processed ice cream that we loved as children, these little cookies are as flavourful as they are nostalgic. One of the friends who taste-tested these said they reminded them of a tube of polos, thanks to their dinky size.

Preheat the oven to 160°C (320°F/gas mark 4) and line two 20 x 30 cm (8 x 12 inch) tins using the cookie lining method.

In the bowl of a stand mixer with the paddle attachment or a large mixing bowl with an electric whisk, cream the butter and caster sugar until pale and fluffy, then add the egg yolk and mix until smooth. Decant half of the mixture into a separate bowl and set aside.

To make the vanilla cookies, add 110 g (3¾ oz/scant 1 cup) of the flour to the first bowl along with the vanilla paste, then mix to a thick dough. If the mixture is too crumbly and doesn't come together, add a teaspoon of milk to loosen it slightly. Wrap in cling film (plastic wrap) and put in the fridge for 20 minutes.

Meanwhile, add the remaining 90 g (3¼ oz/¾ cup) of flour to the second bowl along with the cocoa powder, then mix to a thick dough. If the mixture is too crumbly, add a teaspoon of milk. Wrap in cling film and put in the fridge to firm up for 20 minutes.

When you are ready to bake the cookies, set the vanilla cookie dough on a lightly floured surface, then roll it to a thickness of around 3 mm (⅛ inch). Using a 3 cm (1¼ inch cutter) stamp out rounds and set them in the prepared baking tins. Reroll the dough and repeat until all of the vanilla dough has been used up, then transfer to the oven and bake for 8–10 minutes, until just colouring at the edges. You may need to make them in batches. Transfer the cookies to a wire rack, then repeat the process with the chocolate dough.

While the cookies are cooling, make the buttercream by whisking together the softened butter and icing sugar until smooth and creamy. If the mixture is too thick, add 1–2 teaspoons of milk to loosen. Add the freeze-dried strawberry powder and whisk again to incorporate, then transfer to a piping bag fitted with a round nozzle. If you don't have a piping bag, you can use a teaspoon to fill the cookies. To assemble the cookies, sandwich the vanilla and chocolate cookies with a good dollop of the buttercream. You will get the cleanest finish if you pipe a generous pearl of buttercream onto the centre of one cookie, top with a second cookie and gently press until the buttercream fills to the edges.

PEANUT BUTTER + JAM THUMBPRINT COOKIES

PREP: 25 minutes, plus chilling
COOK: 30 minutes
MAKES: 20–22 cookies

175 g (6 oz/scant 1½ cups)
plain (all-purpose) flour

50 g (2 oz/generous ¼ cup)
light brown soft sugar

½ tsp fine salt

150 g (5 oz/scant ⅔ cup)
smooth peanut butter

2 eggs

milk, if needed

50 g (2 oz/⅓ cup) salted peanuts,
finely chopped (optional)

150 g (5 oz/scant ½ cup)
raspberry jam

NOTES

SHELF LIFE: These will keep
well for up to five days wrapped
tightly in cellophane or stored
in an airtight container.

SUBSTITUTIONS: Use any
jam you like. You can omit the
chopped peanuts, too.

HOW TO POST: Lay two,
four or six cookies on a piece
of cellophane, then carefully
and tightly wrap over the top
to seal. Cushion with tissue paper.
These are best sent on their
own in a snug-fitting box.

*The name thumbprint – adorable, and reminiscent of the tales of
Tom Thumb and Thumbelina – enticed me as soon as I first saw these
stocky little cookies, ready to overflow with jammy filling. My version
draws on the classic American sandwich filling, which, I think, is a
rare example of perfect equilibrium between sweet, sour and salt.*

Preheat the oven to 180°C (350°F/gas mark 6) and line a 20 x 30 cm
(8 x 12 inch) tin with baking parchment on the base only.

Combine the flour, sugar and salt in a large bowl, then add the
peanut butter and crack in the eggs. Beat until well combined. If it feels
a little dry and crumbly, add some milk – one tablespoon at a time –
until the dough is smooth enough to roll into balls without cracking.
Different peanut butters have different liquid contents, which is why
you may need to add this. Then use your hands to roll the mixture into
20–22 walnut-sized balls.

If using the chopped peanuts, put them in a small bowl, then roll
each of the balls of cookie mixture in the peanuts to coat the outer
edge. Lay them in the prepared baking tin (you will need to do this
in batches).

Push the narrow end of a wooden spoon into the centre of
each cookie until you just feel the base of the tin through the cookie.
Twist to widen each hole slightly, then remove the spoon. Put the
cookies in the fridge to firm up for 20 minutes.

Once chilled, bake the cookies for 12–15 minutes, rotating the tin
halfway through the cooking time. Remove the cookies from the oven,
then put a small spoonful of the jam into the indentation in the centre
of each cookie (you can do this with a piping bag if you want to be
extra neat). Return the cookies to the oven for another 5 minutes, then
set aside to cool while you repeat the process with the remaining balls
of cookie dough.

ROSEMARY + WALNUT CRACKERS

PREP: 20 minutes, plus chilling
COOK: 40 minutes–1 hour
MAKES: 30–40 crackers

250 g (9 oz/2 cups)
plain (all-purpose) flour

½ tsp baking powder

½ tsp salt

1 tsp ground black pepper

4–5 sprigs of fresh rosemary,
leaves finely chopped

50 g (2 oz) unsalted butter, cubed

125 ml (4 fl oz/½ cup) cold water

75 g (2½ oz/scant ⅔ cup) finely
chopped walnuts

flaky sea salt, for sprinkling

NOTES

SHELF LIFE: These keep
well for up to a week tightly
wrapped in cellophane or
stored in an airtight container.

SUBSTITUTIONS: You can
add a sprinkling of seeds to
the crackers before baking.

HOW TO POST: Stack the
crackers in a tower and wrap
in cellophane and tissue paper.
These work well in a mixed box.

While nutty, fragrant crackers are a match made in heaven for a slick of membrillo (page 144) and a hunk of creamy blue cheese, the fresh rosemary here brings a richness that makes them delicious to snack on by themselves, too. Instead of traditional rounds, try cutting these into shards or squares for something a little different.

Preheat the oven to 170°C (340°F/gas mark 5) and line a 20 x 30 cm (8 x 12 inch) tin with baking parchment on the base only.

Sift the flour, baking powder and salt into a large bowl, then add the black pepper and chopped rosemary (reserving a little to top the crackers with) and stir to combine. Add the butter to the bowl and use your fingers to rub it into the flour until the mixture resembles fine breadcrumbs. Add the chopped walnuts to the bowl followed by the water, then use your hands to bring the mixture together into a soft dough.

Turn the dough out onto a lightly floured surface and divide into two equal pieces. Wrap one of the pieces of dough in cling film (plastic wrap) and put in the fridge for later. Using a rolling pin, roll the other piece of dough very thinly, until you can almost see the work surface through it.

Using a round 7.5 cm (3 inch) cutter, stamp out rounds of the dough and place them in the prepared tin, leaving a little space between them to spread during cooking. Prick each cracker with a fork, then sprinkle with flaky sea salt and a little fresh rosemary, then put the tin in the fridge for 15 minutes to allow the crackers to firm up.

Once chilled, transfer the tin to the oven and bake the crackers for 20–30 minutes, until golden and crisp. Transfer the crackers to a wire rack to cool, then roll, chill and bake the second half of the dough in the same way.

PARMESAN + CAYENNE PEPPER BISCUITS

PREP: 15 minutes, plus chilling
COOK: 12 minutes
MAKES: 20 biscuits (shortbreads)

75 g (2½ oz/scant ⅔ cup) plain (all-purpose) flour

75 g (2½ oz) fridge-cold unsalted butter, cubed

75 g (2½ oz) Parmesan, finely grated

¼ tsp cayenne pepper

50 g (2 oz/generous ½ cup) flaked (slivered) almonds

NOTES

GET AHEAD: You can make the dough up to the point of wrapping and refrigerating up to two days before baking.

SHELF LIFE: These keep well for up to a week wrapped tightly in cellophane or stored in an airtight container.

SUBSTITUTIONS: Increase, reduce or omit the cayenne, according to personal taste.

HOW TO POST: Stack the biscuits (cookies) in a tower and wrap in cellophane before wrapping in tissue paper. These work well in a mixed box.

Sometimes my sweet tooth (and, frankly, all of my teeth) need a break, and when I crave something deeply savoury, these little cheese biscuits are just the ticket. A classic short Parmesan biscuit dough is elevated with a snap of flaked almonds and a kick of fiery cayenne. If you're braver than my taste testers, try using ½ a teaspoon of cayenne for a little more heat.

To make the dough, put the flour and butter in a large bowl and use the tips of your fingers to rub the butter into the flour, until it is well combined and resembles fine breadcrumbs. Add the Parmesan and cayenne pepper to the bowl and stir briefly to combine, then use your hands to start to bring the mixture together.

Add the flaked almonds to the bowl, then turn out onto a clean work surface and knead gently to combine and mix the nuts through. Once you have a soft dough, roll it into an even sausage shape roughly 4 cm (1½ inches) in diameter (about the size of a milk bottle top). Wrap the sausage in cling film (plastic wrap) and place in the fridge to chill for an hour or so.

When you're ready to bake the biscuits, preheat the oven to 180°C (350°F/gas mark 6), and line a 20 x 30 cm (8 x 12 inch) tin with baking parchment on the base only.

Unwrap the log of dough and carefully slice it into 5 mm (¼ inch) rounds. Spread the biscuits out in the prepared tin, leaving a little space between them to spread during cooking, then transfer to the oven to bake for 10–12 minutes until lightly golden. You may need to bake in batches. Transfer to a wire rack to cool.

COCOA + MACADAMIA SABLES

PREP: 20 minutes, plus chilling
COOK: 15 minutes
MAKES: 20–25 sables

150 g (5 oz/scant 1¼ cups)
plain (all-purpose) flour

25 g (1 oz) cocoa (unsweetened
chocolate) powder

100 g (3½ oz) unsalted butter,
at room temperature

¼ tsp fine salt

100 g (3½ oz/scant ½ cup)
caster (superfine) sugar

1 tsp vanilla extract

1–2 tsp whole milk

100 g (3½ oz/scant ⅔ cup)
macadamia nuts

NOTES

GET AHEAD: Make the sable
dough and store wrapped in the
fridge for up to a week or freezer
for up to a month. Allow the
dough to thaw before baking.

SHELF LIFE: Once baked,
these will keep well for up to 10 days
when wrapped in cling film (plastic
wrap) or in an airtight container.

SUBSTITUTIONS: Swap the
macadamias for almost any nut –
pistachios, almonds and hazelnuts
all work well. To make these nut
free, you could substitute them
for chunks of chocolate.

HOW TO POST: Stack and wrap in
cellophane, then wrap in tissue paper.

Paramount as taste is to me in baking, it would be churlish to deny that we eat with our eyes as much as our mouths. The contrast of the pale, buttery macadamia nuts and the near-black cocoa biscuit dough of these sables is sure to please at all levels.

Quick and easy to make, these are forgiving and welcome substitution, so swap out the nuts for whatever you have. I've recommended a few choice alternatives in the notes below.

Put the flour, cocoa powder, butter, salt, sugar and vanilla extract in the bowl of a stand mixer fitted with a whisk attachment. Mix on a low speed for 5–10 minutes, until it has a moist crumb texture.

Remove the whisk fitting and use your hands to bring the mixture into a dough. If it is too crumbly, add a teaspoon of milk to bind it together.

Add the macadamia nuts to the bowl, then turn out onto a clean work surface and knead gently to combine and mix the nuts through. Split the mixture into two equal-sized balls, then roll each into a sausage shape until it is roughly 4 cm (1½ inches) in diameter (about the size of a milk bottle top). Wrap each of the sausages in cling film (plastic wrap) and place in the fridge to chill for an hour or so.

When you're ready to bake the sables, preheat the oven to 160°C (320°F/gas mark 4), and line two tins with baking parchment on the base only.

Unwrap the logs of sable dough and carefully slice them into 1 cm (½ inch) rounds. Spread the sables out in the prepared tins, leaving a little space between them to spread during cooking, then transfer to the oven to bake for 14–15 minutes. Leave in the tin for 10 minutes to firm up, then transfer to a wire rack to cool fully.

TAHINI + MILK CHOCOLATE COOKIES

PREP: 20 minutes
COOK: 24 minutes
MAKES: 12 cookies

100 g (3½ oz) unsalted butter, soft

150 g (5 oz/generous ¾ cup) dark brown soft sugar

1 egg

1 tsp vanilla bean paste

125 g (4 oz/1 cup) plain (all-purpose) flour

1 tsp bicarbonate of soda (baking soda)

½ tsp fine sea salt

125 g (4 oz/scant ½ cup) tahini

100 g (3½ oz) milk chocolate, finely chopped

flaky sea salt, for sprinkling

20 g (¾ oz) sesame seeds (optional)

NOTES

GET AHEAD: Use an ice cream scoop to portion the cookie dough onto a baking sheet and freeze. Once they are frozen solid you can transfer them to a zip-lock bag and store in the freezer. To bake from frozen, spread out on a lined tray and bake at the same temperature for 15–20 minutes.

SHELF LIFE: These keep well for up to a week wrapped or stored in an airtight container.

SUBSTITUTIONS: Use any chocolate you like – white chocolate also pairs beautifully with tahini.

HOW TO POST: Stack the cookies in a tower and wrap in cellophane and tissue paper. These work well in a mixed box.

These are my go-to cookies when I need to make something quickly. A classic choc chip cookie recipe at its core, it's enriched with a generous dollop of creamy tahini, a sesame seed paste that brings a delicious flavour and unctuous texture to baking. These are also great to make ahead and freeze to bake from frozen at a later date.

Preheat the oven to 180°C (350°F/gas mark 6) and line a 20 x 30 cm (8 x 12 inch) tin with baking parchment on the base only.

In the bowl of a stand mixer with the paddle attachment or a large mixing bowl with an electric whisk, cream the butter and dark brown soft sugar until pale and fluffy, then crack in the egg and add the vanilla and mix again until well combined.

In a separate bowl, combine the flour, bicarbonate of soda and salt, then tip this mixture into the bowl with the butter, sugar and egg and beat until well combined. Add the tahini and beat again.

Measure out 60 g (2 oz) of the milk chocolate and add to the bowl with the cookie dough, then mix well to incorporate the chocolate through the dough. Using an ice cream scoop or tablespoon, scoop mounds of the cookie dough into the prepared tin, leaving a little space between them to spread during cooking (you will need to do this in batches as they won't all fit on one tin).

Sprinkle a little sea salt over each of the cookies, then transfer to the oven to bake for 8–12 minutes, until well spread and starting to crisp at the edges. Leave to cool and firm up in the tin, then transfer to a wire rack and repeat the process for the rest of the cookie dough.

Once all of the cookies are cooked, melt the remaining chocolate in sharp bursts in the microwave, then drizzle it over the cookies. If using the sesame seeds, sprinkle these over while the chocolate is still molten.

CITRUSY PINE NUT AMARETTI

PREP: 20 minutes,
plus resting the dough
COOK: 30 minutes
MAKE: 14–18 amaretti

3 egg whites

280 g (10¼ oz/2¾ cups)
ground almonds

¼ tsp salt

180 g (6¼ oz/generous ¾ cup)
caster (superfine) sugar

zest of 1 lemon

20 g (¾ oz) pine nuts

icing (confectioner's) sugar,
for rolling

NOTES

SHELF LIFE: These keep well
for up to two weeks wrapped
tightly in cellophane or stored
in an airtight container.

SUBSTITUTIONS: Swap the
lemon zest for orange and leave
out the pine nuts, if you prefer.

HOW TO POST: Pack neatly
in a cellophane or greaseproof paper
bag, then wrap in tissue paper.

A traditional amaretti – flavoured only with almonds – is a thing of beauty, and you can make these that way if you prefer by omitting the lemon and pine nuts. I like the fragrance and bite these additions bring and, given that they are two of Italy's best-known exports, I hope they're not too much of a stretch.

In the bowl of a stand mixer with the whisk attachment or a large mixing bowl with an electric whisk, whisk the egg whites until frothy but not yet forming peaks.

In a separate bowl, combine the ground almonds, salt and sugar, then tip this mixture into the bowl with the egg whites and gently fold through with a metal spoon to combine. Add the lemon zest and pine nuts and gently mix through the dough, then cover the bowl with cling film (plastic wrap) and leave the dough to rest and firm up for at least an hour or overnight.

When you are ready to bake the amaretti, preheat the oven to 180°C (350°F/gas mark 6) and line a 20 x 30 cm (8 x 12 inch) tin on the base only.

Put a small plate on the kitchen counter and spread a layer of icing sugar over it. Using your hands, roll walnut-sized balls of the amaretti dough, then roll in the icing sugar to coat. Place in the prepared tin, spacing them out to allow them to spread during cooking, while you form and coat the other amaretti (you will need to do this in batches or use two tins).

Once the amaretti are formed, gently press down on their tops to flatten slightly – you don't want to squash them, but flattening the tops will aid the formation of their signature cracks in the oven. Transfer to the oven and bake for 12–15 minutes, until puffed up and just firm to the touch.

RYE + APRICOT BISCOTTI

PREP: 20 minutes, plus cooling
COOK: 55 minutes
MAKES: 20–25 biscotti

150 g (5 oz/scant 1 cup) whole, skin-on almonds

175 g (6 oz/generous ¾ cup) caster (superfine) sugar

2 eggs

zest of 2 oranges

250 g (9 oz/2½ cups) rye flour

½ tsp salt

½ tsp baking powder

200 g (7 oz/generous 1 cup) dried apricots, roughly chopped

150 g (5 oz) dark or white chocolate (optional)

NOTES

SHELF LIFE: These keep well for up to two weeks wrapped tightly or stored in an airtight container.

SUBSTITUTIONS: Use any nuts or dried fruit you like. You can also replace the rye with plain (all-purpose) flour, if you prefer.

HOW TO POST: Pack the biscotti neatly in a cellophane or greaseproof paper bag, then wrap in tissue paper.

Biscotti are designed for dunking, but I love biscotti on their own just as much as I like them with my coffee. My recipe uses rye flour for a darker result and a deeper flavour.

Preheat the oven to 180°C (350°F/gas mark 6) and line a 20 x 30 cm (8 x 12 inch) tin with baking parchment on the base only.

Spread the almonds out in the tin and roast in the oven for 10–15 minutes until they have darkened slightly and are lightly fragrant. Remove from the oven and set aside to cool.

In the bowl of a stand mixer with the whisk attachment or a large mixing bowl with an electric whisk, whisk the caster sugar and eggs for 4–5 minutes, until the mixture is very pale and has doubled in volume. Stir through the orange zest.

In a separate bowl, combine the flour, salt and baking powder, then sift this over the egg mixture and gently fold through. Add the almonds and apricots to the bowl, mix to combine, then turn the mixture out onto a lightly floured surface and use your hands to bring it into a dough.

Split the dough into two halves, then roll each half into an even cylinder measuring approximately 5 x 30 cm (2 x 12 inches). Transfer the logs to the baking tin and bake for 25–30 minutes, until the dough has risen and cracks have formed on the surface.

Remove the biscotti from the oven and reduce the oven temperature to 160°C (320°F/gas mark 4). Set the biscotti aside to cool for 30 minutes, them use a sharp, heavy knife to carefully slice thin biscuits from the baked dough. Lay these out in the tin (you may need to do this in several batches), and return to the oven to bake for a further 10–15 minutes. The biscotti are baked when they are cooked through and firm at the centre.

Melt the chocolate in a bowl, if using, then dip the biscotti in one at a time and leave to set.

DIY ICED VANILLA BISCUIT BOX

PREP: 15 minutes
COOK: 12 minutes
MAKES: 20–30 biscuits (cookies)

FOR THE BISCUIT DOUGH:

225 g (8 oz) unsalted butter, soft

200 g (7 oz/scant 1 cup) caster (superfine) sugar

1 egg

400 g (14 oz/generous 3 cups) plain (all-purpose) flour

½ tsp salt

1 tsp vanilla bean paste

TO DECORATE:

1 x quantity Royal Icing (page 149)

edible pressed flowers (page 146)

NOTES

GET AHEAD: Make the dough, wrap in cling film (plastic wrap), and refrigerate for up to three days, or freeze for up to two months.

SHELF LIFE: These keep well for up to five days tightly wrapped or stored in an airtight container.

SUBSTITUTIONS: Add the zest of an orange or lemon for citrusy biscuits. Adding the crushed seeds of three cardamom pods is also delicious.

HOW TO POST: Uniced, stack the biscuits (cookies) in a small tower and wrap in cellophane and tissue paper. Pack in a box with Royal Icing and edible flowers for your recipient to decorate at home.

This is a simple biscuit dough which can be made ahead and stored until you are ready to bake your biscuits (see below notes). Sending the biscuits undecorated with icing and pressed flowers makes a sweet gift and is perfect for children – sprinkles could be added instead of pressed flowers for smaller recipients!

Preheat the oven to 180°C (350°F/gas mark 6) and line a 20 x 30 cm (8 x 12 inch) tin with baking parchment on the base only.

In the bowl of a stand mixer with the paddle attachment or a large mixing bowl with an electric whisk, cream the butter and caster sugar until pale and fluffy, then add the egg and beat until smooth. Add the flour, salt and vanilla bean paste and mix to a soft dough.

Turn the dough out onto a lightly-floured surface and knead slightly to bring everything together. At this stage, you can either wrap the dough in cling film (plastic wrap) and chill until you are ready to bake the biscuits, or proceed with rolling them straight away.

Using a rolling pin, roll the dough out to a thickness of 5 mm (¼ inch) and stamp out your choice of shapes, rerolling the scraps of dough until it is all used up. Spread the biscuits out in the prepared tin, leaving a little space between them, and bake for 10–12 minutes, until pale but just starting to turn golden at the edges. Cool fully before icing or packing.

DIY GINGERBREAD BOX

PREP: 15 minutes, plus chilling
COOK: 12 minutes
MAKES: 20–30 biscuits (cookies)

FOR THE BISCUITS:
90 g (3¼ oz) unsalted butter, cubed

110 g (3¾ oz/scant ⅔ cup)
light brown soft sugar

1 egg

80 g (3 oz/scant ¼ cup) treacle

40 g (1½ oz) golden (light corn) syrup

450 g (1 lb/scant 3⅔ cups)
plain (all-purpose) flour

½ tsp salt

3 tsp ground ginger

2 tsp ground cinnamon

1½ tsp ground allspice

a few gratings of nutmeg

TO DECORATE:
1 x quantity Royal Icing (page 149)

sweets, sprinkles and
chocolate buttons

NOTES

GET AHEAD: Make the dough,
wrap in cling film (plastic wrap),
and refrigerate for up to three days,
or freeze for up to two months.

SHELF LIFE: These keep well
for up to a week wrapped tightly
or stored in an airtight container.

HOW TO POST: Uniced, stack
the biscuits (cookies) in a small tower
and wrap in cellophane and tissue
paper. Pack in a box with Royal Icing
and sweets or sprinkles for your
recipient to decorate at home.

This is my no-spread gingerbread recipe, which I developed a few years ago to make 200 French bulldog-shaped gingerbread biscuits for a bespoke order. It's perfect for getting a sharp edge, as it doesn't expand when baking. It would also work for a gingerbread house pattern.

In the bowl of a stand mixer with the paddle attachment or a large mixing bowl with an electric whisk, cream the butter and light brown soft sugar until light and fluffy, then add the egg and beat until smooth. Add the treacle and golden syrup and mix again to combine.

In a separate bowl, combine the flour, salt, ginger, cinnamon, allspice and nutmeg, then tip this mixture into the bowl with the butter, sugar and egg and mix slowly until well combined.

Turn the dough out onto a lightly floured surface and knead slightly to bring everything together. Wrap the dough in cling film (plastic wrap) and chill for at least an hour, or until you are ready to bake the biscuits.

When you are ready to bake the biscuits, preheat the oven to 180°C (350°F/gas mark 6) and line a 20 x 30 cm (8 x 12 inch) tin on the base only.

Unwrap the dough and cut it into quarters, then working with a quarter at a time use a rolling pin to roll the dough out to a thickness of 5 mm (¼ inch) and stamp out your choice of shapes, rerolling the scraps of dough until it is all used up. You can repeat the process with the other pieces of dough or transfer them to the freezer for up to 2 months to use at a later date.

Spread the biscuits out in the prepared baking tin, leaving a little space between them, and bake for 10–12 minutes, until just firm to the touch. Cool fully before icing or packaging.

CONFECTIONERY

CONFECTIONERY

Caramelised White Chocolate Fudge

Grown-Up Chocolate Buttons

Hazelnut + Honey Nougat

Orange Blossom Marshmallows

Peppermint Creams

Raspberry Fruit Pastilles

Salted Caramel Chocolate Truffles

Bonfire Toffee

FROM THE TOWERING JARS OF JEWEL-LIKE CANDY IN CORNER SHOPS TO THE DECADENT PARISIAN DISPLAYS OF NOUGAT AND PÂTES DE FRUITS, I HAVE ALWAYS BEEN OBSESSED WITH CONFECTIONERY.

Anywhere where the air smells like sugar and your teeth stick together is a home from home to me. Thankfully, sweet-making is not as difficult as modern mythology would have us believe – arm yourself with a digital sugar thermometer, say a quiet apology to your teeth and put your best foot forward.

CARAMELISED WHITE CHOCOLATE FUDGE

PREP: 10 minutes, plus setting
COOK: 1 hour 20 minutes
MAKES: 32 pieces

175 g (6 oz) white chocolate, broken into small pieces

470 g (1 lb 1 oz/generous 2 cups) caster (superfine) sugar

125 g (4 oz) liquid glucose

250 g (9 oz/generous 1 cup) double (heavy) cream

65 g (2¼ oz) unsalted butter

1 tsp fine sea salt

NOTES

GET AHEAD: Caramelise the white chocolate a few days before you make the fudge and store in an airtight container until needed.

SHELF LIFE: These will keep well for at least a week.

SUBSTITUTIONS: You can add a tablespoon or two of rum to the fudge when it's cooking, ensuring that it gets back up to 116°C (240°F) afterwards.

HOW TO POST: Pack tightly in a single layer, sliced or as a slab, then wrap in cellophane and tissue paper.

This makes a delicious present and posts brilliantly. If you're feeling keen, pick four or five recipes from this chapter, make them all, and then pack everything up in small packages so that each of your recipients gets their own little homemade sweet shop in the post.

Preheat the oven to 120°C (250°F/gas mark 1) and line two 20 x 30 cm (8 x 12 inch) tins with baking parchment following the traybake method on page 12.

To caramelise the white chocolate, spread the chocolate out evenly in one of the prepared tins. Bake for 10 minutes, then remove the tin from the oven and spread the melted chocolate around with a clean, dry spatula. Continue this process at 10-minute intervals for 40–60 minutes, until the chocolate is a deep, golden caramel colour. Set aside to firm up while you start to make the fudge.

To make the fudge, put the sugar, glucose and double (heavy) cream in a heavy-based saucepan fitted with a sugar thermometer over a medium heat. Cook, stirring occasionally, until the sugar has dissolved, then raise the temperature to high and cook until the mixture reaches 116°C (240°F).

Add the butter, salt and the caramelised white chocolate to the pan, cooking until both ingredients have melted and the temperature has again reached 116°C (240°F). Carefully pour the fudge into the second prepared tin, then leave for 3–4 hours to set at room temperature. Slice and serve.

GROWN-UP
CHOCOLATE BUTTONS

PREP: 10 minutes, plus setting
MAKES: 40 buttons

150 g (5 oz) good-quality
dark chocolate (minimum
70% cocoa solids)

1 tsp flaky sea salt

a section of toppings, such as:
pistachio slivers, dried rose petals,
chopped stem ginger, dried fruits
or sprinkles

NOTES

SHELF LIFE: These will keep
well for up to two weeks.

SUBSTITUTIONS: Use whatever
toppings you have to hand.
You could make these using milk
or white chocolate, too.

POSTING: Pack the buttons
in a small cellophane bag, seal
with tape, then wrap gently in tissue
paper. If sending in a mixed box,
pack these at the top.

*Less of a recipe and more of an idea, these chocolate buttons or
Mendiants are an easy gift to make and perfect for using up odds
and ends lurking at the back of the baking cupboard.*

*Don't be tempted to melt the chocolate over a high heat or set
these in the fridge, as the rapid change in temperature may cause
the chocolate to bloom, which is when little white marks appear
on the surface.*

Line a 20 x 30 cm (8 x 12 inch) tin with baking parchment on the
base only.

To melt the chocolate, bring a pan of water to a gentle simmer
and set a snug-fitting heatproof bowl over the top, ensuring that the
water in the pan doesn't touch the base of the bowl. Add the chocolate
to the bowl and heat, without stirring, until about half the chocolate
has melted, then remove the bowl from the pan and stir until melted.
If not all of the chocolate quite melts, return the bowl to the pan and
heat gently for another 5 minutes before removing and stirring again.

Pour the chocolate into a piping bag with a small round tip,
then pipe small pools of chocolate onto the baking parchment in the
tin until you have used up all of the chocolate. Sprinkle the chocolate
with a little sea salt, then scatter over your choice of toppings.

Leave the buttons to set firm at room temperature.

HAZELNUT + HONEY NOUGAT

PREP: 20 minutes,
plus cooling and setting
COOK: 25 minutes
MAKES: 16 bars
or 48 smaller squares

150 g (5 oz/generous 1 cup)
blanched hazelnuts

300 g (11 oz/scant 1⅓ cups)
caster (superfine) sugar

75 g (2½ oz) liquid glucose

150 ml (5 fl oz/scant ⅔ cup) water

2 egg whites

90 g (3¼ oz/¼ cup) runny honey

½ tsp fine sea salt

50 g (2 oz) glacé cherries (optional)

icing (confectioner's) sugar,
for dusting

NOTES

SHELF LIFE: These will keep
well for at least a week.

SUBSTITUTIONS: Swap the
hazelnuts for other hard nuts
(almonds also work well).
Fold through 100 g (3½ oz)
of melted dark chocolate at the
same time as adding the nuts
to create a marbled nougat.

HOW TO POST: Wrap the pieces
individually in baking parchment,
or wrap a small slab tightly in
cellophane and tissue.

Nougat makes a fantastic gift. If you have the patience, you could individually wrap the sliced pieces in rectangles of baking parchment, like old-fashioned toffees. If not, a sliced slab will go down just as well!

Preheat the oven to 180°C (350°F/gas mark 6), line a 20 x 30 cm (8 x 12 inch) tin following the instructions on page 12 and line a separate baking sheet with parchment.

Spread the hazelnuts on the baking sheet and toast in the oven for 10 minutes, until fragrant and starting to brown. Set aside.

Reserve 1 tablespoon of the sugar then put the remainder in a heavy-based saucepan fitted with a sugar thermometer along with the liquid glucose and water. Set the pan over a medium heat, bring to a boil and leave to cook until the temperature reaches 135°C (275°F).

While the sugar mixture is cooking, put the egg whites and reserved sugar in the bowl of a stand mixer fitted with a whisk attachment and whisk to stiff peaks. Turn off the mixer, but keep the bowl attached.

As soon as the sugar mixture reaches 135°C (275°F) add the honey and salt to the pan and stir quickly to combine. Continue to cook until the mixture reaches 145°C (293°F), then turn on the mixer to a low speed and carefully pour the hot sugar mixture over the whisked egg whites. Once the sugar has been added, turn the speed up to high and continue to whisk for 5–10 minutes, or until the mixture has cooled to room temperature.

Add the hazelnuts and glacé cherries (optional) to the nougat mixture and stir through to incorporate, then tip the mixture into the prepared tin. Press a sheet of baking parchment over the top of the nougat in the tin, then use a rolling pin to spread the nougat out in an even layer.

Leave the nougat to cool to room temperature and set, then slice into bars or smaller squares and dust in icing sugar.

ORANGE BLOSSOM MARSHMALLOWS

PREP: 20 minutes, plus cooling and setting
COOK: 15 minutes
MAKES: 24 marshmallows

vegetable oil, for greasing

125 g (4 oz/1 cup) cornflour (corn starch)

100 g (3½ oz/generous ¾ cup) icing (confectioner's) sugar

350 ml (12 fl oz/scant 1½ cups) water

36 g (1¼ oz/3 sachets) powdered gelatine

500 g (1 lb 2 oz/generous 2 cups) caster (superfine) sugar

50 g (2 oz) liquid glucose

2 egg whites

3 tsp orange blossom water

zest of 1 small orange

NOTES

SHELF LIFE: These keep for up to four days so are best sent using next-day postal services.

SUBSTITUTIONS: Swap the orange blossom water for any flavour extract you prefer. You can also add cocoa (unsweetened chocolate) powder to the dusting for a chocolatey finish.

HOW TO POST: Pack the marshmallows tightly in a single layer, wrapped in cellophane then tissue paper. If sending a mixed box, pack these near to the top to avoid them getting squashed.

Delicious as these are to eat straight from the box, you can also toast them and sandwich between biscuits (cookies) to make s'mores or float a piece atop a freshly made hot chocolate. The latter is my serving style of choice, especially if it's a Parisian-style hot chocolate: thick, full of cream and closer to a sauce than a drink in texture.

Grease a 20 x 30 cm (8 x 12 inch) tin with vegetable oil. Sift the cornflour and icing sugar into a bowl, then pour into the oiled tin and shake to coat the base and sides. Shake any excess back into the bowl, then set aside.

Heat 100 ml (3½ fl oz/scant ½ cup) of the water in a small pan over a low heat until almost boiling, then remove from the heat and sprinkle in the gelatine. Stir to dissolve, then set aside.

Put the caster sugar, liquid glucose and remaining 250 ml (8½ fl oz/generous 1 cup) of water in a heavy-based saucepan fitted with a sugar thermometer. Set the pan over a low heat, until the sugar has dissolved and you can't see any grains when you tilt the pan, then increase the heat to medium and leave to bubble, watching the thermometer carefully, until the temperature reaches 125°C (257°F).

Immediately remove the pan from the heat, pour in the dissolved gelatine and stir well to combine. Set the mixture aside.

Put the egg whites in the bowl of a stand mixer with a whisk attached and whisk on high until they are completely stiff. With the mixer still running, slowly pour in the hot sugar syrup in a steady, gentle trickle. Once all of the liquid has been added, add the orange blossom water and orange zest and keep whisking the mixture for around 10 minutes, until really thick and voluminous.

Pour the marshmallow mixture into the prepared tin, level with a spatula and then gently dust the top with the remaining cornflour and icing sugar mixture. Allow the marshmallow to set at room temperature for a couple of hours, then cut into squares with a heavy knife wiped with a little oil (this will give you a clean cut).

PEPPERMINT CREAMS

PREP: 10 minutes, plus drying
MAKES: 50–60 creams

1 egg white

500 g (1 lb 2 oz/4 cups) icing (confectioner's) sugar, plus extra for dusting

1 tbsp lemon juice

2–3 tsp peppermint essence

gel food colouring (optional)

NOTES

SHELF LIFE: These keep well for up to a week tightly wrapped or stored in an airtight container.

SUBSTITUTIONS: Swap the peppermint essence for violet, rose or orange essence to make different flavoured creams.

HOW TO POST: Pack in a small cellophane bag, seal with tape, then wrap gently in tissue paper. If sending in a mixed box, pack these at the top.

When we were young, my siblings and I made these with our mum over the festive season. One year, her efforts to colour them a subtle mint green were scuppered by impatient small hands, and we spent the holidays eating our way through a box of bright green creams that were deemed too garish to gift.

Line a 20 x 30 cm (8 x 12 inch) tin with baking parchment on the base only.

Put the egg white in the bowl of a stand mixer with a whisk attached and whisk on high until you have stiff peaks. With the mixer still running, slowly add the icing sugar, lemon juice and peppermint essence, tasting the mixture after each teaspoon of peppermint essence is added until you are happy with the flavour.

If you are colouring your peppermint creams, divide the mixture between as many bowls as colours you want to make and stir a little of the gel colouring through each batch of mixture.

Dust the counter with plenty of icing sugar, then turn the peppermint mixture out onto it. Dust a rolling pin with icing sugar, then roll out the mixture thinly. Use a round 3–4 cm (1¼–1½ inch) cutter to stamp out rounds of the mixture, then place them in your lined tin. Leave in a warm, dry place (an airing cupboard works well) to dry for 3–4 hours or overnight. Store out of the fridge in an airtight container.

RASPBERRY FRUIT PASTILLES

PREP: 10 minutes,
plus cooling and setting
COOK: 15 minutes
MAKES: 48 pastilles

900 g (2 lb) raspberries

750 g (1 lb 9 oz/3¼ cups)
caster (superfine) sugar,
plus 100 g (3½ oz/scant ½ cup)
extra for dusting

50 g (1¾ oz) pectin powder

NOTES

SHELF LIFE: These keep for
up to a week wrapped tightly
or stored in an airtight container.

HOW TO POST: Pack these
tightly in a single layer, wrapped
in cellophane then tissue paper.
If sending a mixed box, pack
these near the top to avoid them
getting squashed.

These pastilles are really Pâtes de Fruits, a traditional French set fruit paste brought out with the petit four at the end of a meal. Rue du Bac, one of my favourite streets in Paris and home to a number of the city's finest patisseries, sells the best. Whenever I visit the city, I return with boxes of glittering, immaculately packed Pâtes de Fruits crammed into every spare inch of space. They are the perfect gift, although I can't promise they always make it to their intended recipient. These pastilles are my homage to that little taste of Paris.

Line a 20 x 30 cm (8 x 12 inch) tin following the instructions on page 12 for the cling film (plastic wrap) method, using kitchen clips to hold the sides in place.

Put the raspberries into the jug of a blender and blend until smooth. Set a sieve (strainer) over a non-stick pan and pass the raspberry purée through to remove the seeds.

Add the sugar and pectin powder to the purée, stir well to combine, then set over a medium heat. Use a sugar thermometer to monitor the temperature, and bring to the boil, stirring regularly until really thick. Once the mixture reaches 104°C (220°F), remove from the heat and pour into the prepared tin.

Set the tin aside until the mixture has cooled to room temperature and completely set, then slice into squares and toss in the extra sugar to coat.

SALTED CARAMEL CHOCOLATE TRUFFLES

PREP: 10 minutes, plus making the salted caramel, setting and chilling
COOK: 10 minutes
MAKES: 40–50 truffles

400 g (14 oz) salted caramel (page 145)

400 g (14 oz) dark chocolate (minimum 70% cocoa solids), broken into small pieces

flaky sea salt

cocoa (unsweetened chocolate) powder, for rolling

NOTES

SHELF LIFE: These keep for up to a week wrapped tightly or stored in an airtight container.

SUBSTITUTIONS: Add the zest of an orange to the mixture, or you can dip the rolled truffles in melted chocolate for a different finish (just allow to set before packing).

HOW TO POST: Pack the truffles in a small cellophane bag, seal with tape, then wrap gently in tissue paper. If sending in a mixed box, pack these at the top.

These truffles are so easy to make and are the perfect way to use up leftover caramel (if such a thing exists). If you prefer, you can roll them in chopped nuts or desiccated coconut, or spear with a fork and dunk into melted chocolate for an extra flourish. I rather love the way the cocoa powder coating looks, dusty and a little imperfect.

Line a 20 x 30 cm (8 x 12 inch) tin with cling film (plastic wrap).

Put the salted caramel in a pan over a medium heat until it starts to bubble. Remove the pan from the heat and add the chocolate. Leave for 30 seconds, then stir the chocolate through the caramel – it should quickly melt, blend with the caramel and become smooth.

Tip the mixture into the prepared tin and level out with a spatula. Sprinkle some flaky sea salt over the surface, then set aside to cool to room temperature. Once cool, transfer to the fridge to set fully for 1–2 hours.

Once the truffle mixture is fully set, place a small plate on the counter and dust it liberally with cocoa powder. Cut the truffle mixture into small triangles, or roll spoonfuls into small balls with your hands, then roll in the cocoa powder to coat. Continue until all of the truffle mixture is used up.

BONFIRE TOFFEE

PREP: 10 minutes,
plus cooling and setting
COOK: 15 minutes
MAKES: 10–20 pieces

175 g (6 oz/scant 1 cup)
dark brown soft sugar

5 tbsp water

50 g (2 oz) unsalted butter

100 g (3½ oz/generous ¼ cup)
golden (light corn) syrup

100g (3½ oz/generous ¼ cup)
black treacle

½ tsp fine sea salt

NOTES

SHELF LIFE: The toffee starts
to get sticky if it is exposed to air,
so wrap tightly in baking parchment
or store in an airtight container as
soon as it has fully cooled. It is best
consumed within a few days of
making, so send out using next-day
postal services.

HOW TO POST: Wrap a slab
in cellophane or baking parchment,
followed by tissue paper. Send with
a mini toffee hammer enclosed so
your recipient can break up the
pieces themselves.

*Is it even bonfire night if you don't spend the evening with your teeth
glued together with toffee? The taste of this dark, bittersweet toffee
conjures up crackling bonfires, cold noses, hot dogs and mud-logged
wellies, and makes the perfect winter treat. If you're sending the toffee
to a friend, top the box with a toffee hammer so your recipient can
crack their own piece from the slab.*

Line a 20 x 30 cm (8 x 12 inch) tin following the instructions on page 12,
using kitchen clips to hold the sides in place. Oil the parchment
generously to ensure that the toffee doesn't stick to it.

 Put all of the ingredients into a non-stick saucepan with a
sugar thermometer attached, then set over a medium heat, stirring
occasionally, until the butter has melted and the sugar has dissolved.

 Then, increase the heat to a rolling boil, and cook until the mixture
reaches hard crack stage (150°C/302°/gas mark 2), which should take
around 5–10 minutes. Carefully pour the hot toffee into the prepared tin.
Leave to cool completely and set solid.

 Once cooled, use a toffee hammer or rolling pin to break the toffee
into shards. Store in an airtight container for up to a week.

STORECUPBOARD STAPLES

STORECUPBOARD STAPLES

Raspberry Curd

Lemon Curd

Passionfruit Curd

Maple, Coconut + Cardamom Granola

Quince Membrillo

Salted Caramel

Pressed Edible Flowers

Crystallised Rose Petals

Honeycomb

Royal Icing

WELCOME TO YOUR NEW-AGE STORE-CUPBOARD. THIS CHAPTER IS FILLED WITH RECIPES THAT HAVE BECOME STAPLES IN MY KITCHEN AND HAVE A PLETHORA OF USES IN BAKING.

Most of these recipes are not designed to be posted as they are; rather, they are helpful elements to make and use in your baking, and you will find them all used in recipes throughout this book.

RASPBERRY CURD

PREP: 5 minutes, plus cooling
COOK: 15 minutes
MAKES: 2–3 small jars

300 g (10½ oz) raspberries

50 g (2 oz/scant ¼ cup)
caster (superfine) sugar

juice of ½ lemon

2 eggs, lightly beaten

50 g (2 oz) unsalted butter, cubed

Put the raspberries into the jug of a blender and blend until smooth. Set a sieve (strainer) over a non-stick pan and pass the raspberry purée through to remove the seeds. Add the sugar and lemon juice to the pan and place over a medium heat, stirring occasionally, until just starting to bubble.

Reduce the heat to low, then crack in the eggs and whisk to combine. Continue to cook, whisking continuously, until the mixture thickens and coats the back of a spoon. Remove from the heat and add the butter, continuing to whisk until the butter has melted and incorporated fully into the curd.

Decant the mixture into sterilised jars and leave to cool completely before using. In a sealed jar, this will keep in the fridge for up to 2 weeks.

LEMON CURD

PREP: 5 minutes, plus cooling
COOK: 15 minutes
MAKES: 2–3 small jars

juice of 4 lemons

120 g (4 oz/generous ½ cup)
caster sugar

80 g (3 oz) unsalted butter, cubed

4 eggs, lightly beaten

Heat the lemon juice, sugar and butter in a small pan over a low heat, stirring occasionally, until the butter melts.

Crack the eggs into the pan and whisk to combine. Continue to cook over a low heat, whisking continuously, for 10–12 minutes, until the mixture thickens and coats the back of a spoon.

Remove from the heat and strain through a sieve (strainer) into a jug, then decant into sterilised jars. Leave to cool completely before using. In a sealed jar, this will keep in the fridge for up to 2 weeks.

PASSIONFRUIT CURD

PREP: 5 minutes, plus cooling
COOK: 15 minutes
MAKES: 2–3 small jars

250 g (9 oz) passionfruit flesh
(about 12 fruit)

juice of 1 lemon

100 g (3½ oz/scant ½ cup)
caster (superfine) sugar

100 g (3½ oz) unsalted butter, cubed

4 eggs, lightly beaten

Halve the passionfruits, scoop the flesh into the jug of a blender and blend until smooth. Set a sieve (strainer) over a non-stick pan and pass the passionfruit purée through to remove the seeds (don't worry if a few sneak through). Add the lemon juice, sugar and butter to the pan and place over a low heat, stirring occasionally, until the butter melts.

Crack the eggs into the pan and whisk to combine. Continue to cook over a low heat, whisking continuously, for 10–12 minutes, until the mixture thickens and coats the back of a spoon. Leave to cool completely before using. In a sealed jar, this will keep in the fridge for up to 2 weeks.

FRUIT CURDS

I use a lot of fruit curds in my cakes. I prefer
them to jam as I find they bring a welcome
sharpness which contrasts with sweet sponge
and sugary buttercream. When testing the
recipes for this book I found myself reaching
for curds again and again, once more looking
for a sour note for balance.

Each of these recipes will fill two to three
jars, depending on their size. I prefer fruit
curds on the sharp side, so use less sugar than
in many recipes.

MAPLE, COCONUT + CARDAMOM GRANOLA

PREP: 10 minutes, plus cooling
COOK: 30 minutes
MAKES: 1 large jar

40 g (1½ oz) coconut oil, melted

250 g (9 oz/2½ cups) rolled oats

75 g (2½ oz) maple syrup

seeds from 6–12 cardamom pods, crushed

100 g (3½ oz/scant ¾ cup) skin-on hazelnuts or pistachios

40 g (1½ oz) coconut chips

100 g (3½ oz) dried fruit (apricots, cranberries, sultanas or figs all work well)

dried rose petals (optional)

NOTES

SHELF LIFE: The granola will keep well for up to a month in an airtight container.

SUBSTITUTIONS: Swap the fruit and nuts for whatever you have to hand. You can also use agave syrup in place of maple.

HOW TO POST: Pack in a greaseproof paper bag, then wrap in tissue paper. The granola will happily travel in a mixed box or by itself in a snug-fitting box.

I'd like to say that I eat my granola with thick yoghurt, seasonal fruit and honey – and occasionally I do – but usually I eat it with my hands straight out of the jar, standing in my kitchen willing my coffee machine to heat up faster, and cutting it painfully fine to make my bus. The cardamom brings a heady warmth which I welcome and, frankly, need first thing in the morning.

I prefer my granola to have thick clumps of sweet baked oats – perhaps because of the aforementioned kitchen grazing – but you can skip the pressing stage if you like a looser texture. I use a lot of cardamom because I love the flavour, but you can use a little less if you like a subtler warmth.

Preheat the oven to 180°C (350°F/gas mark 6) and line a 20 x 30 cm (8 x 12 inch) tin following the instructions on page 12.

Combine the coconut oil, oats, maple syrup and cardamom in a large bowl and mix until the oats are well coated in the oil and syrup. Using your hands, clump some of the mixture together to create pockets of texture in the granola, then add the hazelnuts and coconut chips to the bowl and stir to combine.

Tip the mixture into the prepared tin and transfer to the oven to bake for 20–30 minutes, mixing with a fork halfway through the cooking time, until crisp and golden. Set aside to cool and harden in the tin, then mix through the dried fruit and transfer to an airtight container.

QUINCE MEMBRILLO

PREP: 15 minutes,
plus cooling and setting
COOK: 2 hours 40 minutes
MAKES: 8 slabs of membrillo

900 g (2 lbs) quince
(about three whole fruits),
washed, cored and chopped
into small pieces

1 orange

1 lemon

about 600 g (1 lb 5 oz/scant 2⅔ cups)
caster (superfine) sugar, plus extra
for dusting

NOTES

SHELF LIFE: Wrapped in
cling film (plastic wrap) and
stored in the fridge, membrillo
will keep for at least six months.

POSTING: Wrap tightly in
cellophane or baking parchment
and tissue. Post in a mixed box
or on its own in a snug-fitting
container. Pack up with the
Rosemary + Walnut Crackers
(page 104) or the Parmesan +
Cayenne Pepper Biscuits
(page 106) so your recipient
just needs to add cheese.

Also called quince cheese, this is a thick fruit paste that is utterly delicious served with, well, cheese. Quince – gnarly, blossomy and aromatic – proves divisive; my grandparents grow great gluts every year and, as it is the one fruit my grandad cannot stand, my granny has become most inventive with uses for it over the years. Membrillo is a family favourite, and can either be served with cheese and cold cuts or sliced and coated in sugar to make fruit pastilles.

Line a 20 x 30 cm (8 x 12 inch) tin with 3 layers of cling film (plastic wrap) and set aside.

Put the chopped quince in a large pan with enough water to completely cover the fruit. Use a vegetable peeler to pare the zest from the orange and lemon and add it to the pan. Juice the orange and lemon and add that too.

Bring the mixture to a gentle simmer, then cook over a low heat for 1 hour 30 minutes–2 hours, stirring regularly, until the quince has broken down and the water has turned pink.

Remove and discard the citrus zest, then use a stick (immersion) blender to blend the mixture to a smooth purée. Set a large bowl on a set of weighing scales and pour in the purée to weigh it – you should have between 900 g (2 lbs) and 1 kg (2 lbs 4 oz). Return the quince purée to the pan along with two-thirds of its total weight of sugar (so, for 900 g (2 lbs) of purée you would add 600 g (1 lb 5 oz) of sugar).

Place the pan over a medium heat and stir well to incorporate the sugar, then cook the mixture, stirring occasionally, for 30–40 minutes, until it is very thick and coats the back of a spoon.

Pour the mixture into the prepared baking tin and leave until cool and fully set at room temperature before removing from the tin and slicing.

SALTED CARAMEL

PREP: 5 minutes, plus cooling
COOK: 15 minutes
MAKES: 2–3 small jars

360 g (12½ oz/generous 1½ cups) caster (superfine) sugar

300 ml (10 fl oz/1¼ cups) double (heavy) cream

60 g (2 oz) unsalted butter

2½ tsp fine sea salt

This makes a thick, unctuous salted caramel sauce which is incredibly versatile. While it features in a number of recipes in this book, you could just as easily heat it up and serve it with ice cream or pour it over a sticky toffee pudding. A pretty jar of caramel – tied with a ribbon – makes a sweet gift in itself.

At the height of the brownie hustle, I was making four times the quantity of the recipe below twice a week. If you also have high caramel needs, it is easily scaled up and will keep in jars in the fridge for at least two months.

Put the sugar in a heavy-based, squeaky-clean saucepan over a medium-low heat. Cook the sugar without stirring (as this can cause the sugar to crystallise) until it has dissolved. If it needs a bit of encouragement to dissolve evenly, gently shake the pan to move the sugar around. Once the sugar has all melted, you can gently whisk it to encourage even browning.

Once the caramel is a deep golden brown, remove the pan from the heat and pour in the cream. Being careful (it will bubble), whisk the mixture to combine. If any lumps of caramel solidify, return the pan to a gentle heat and stir to melt through. Add the butter and salt, stir to melt, and then carefully pour into sterilised jars. Leave to cool before using.

PRESSED EDIBLE FLOWERS

PREP: 10 minutes,
plus several days resting
MAKES: as many as you like

a selection of fresh, dry and
just-bloomed edible flowers

blotting paper

newspaper

a stack of heavy books

Pressing flowers is much easier than most people think. If you are using pressed flowers to decorate biscuits, you must ensure they are edible (www.rhs.org.uk is a great resource for identifying which to use and which to avoid).

Once pressed, the flowers will keep indefinitely, although will fade in colour the longer they are stored.

Open a large, heavy book near the centre and lay a sheet of newspaper on one of the pages. Top the newspaper with a sheet of blotting paper, then spread a selection of flowers out over the sheet, placing flower heads face-side down and stemmed flowers on their sides. Top the flowers with a second sheet of blotting paper followed by a second sheet of newspaper. Repeat this process at intervals throughout the book.

Once you have arranged all of your flowers, close the book and stack a pile of other heavy books on top to weigh it down. Leave in a cool, dry place (an airing cupboard or by a radiator works well) and check on the progress of the flowers daily. Depending on the size of the flowers and warmth of your drying location, they can take anywhere between three days and two weeks to dry.

CRYSTALLISED ROSE PETALS

PREP: Prep: 10 minutes,
plus drying time
MAKES: as many as you like

a selection of fresh, clean
and dry rose petals

1 egg white

caster (superfine) sugar

NOTES

HOW TO POST: Place in a small cellophane bag, seal, and wrap well in tissue paper. Place at the top of the box to avoid them getting crushed.

These are easy to make and a great form of edible decoration for your bakes. I use these to decorate my Raspberry + Rose Brownies (page 27), but they can also be packed up in a cellophane bag and sent as their own edible treat.

Carefully separate the rose petals. Next, whisk the egg white with a fork until foamy but not yet forming peaks. Place a thick layer of sugar on a plate and set aside.

Use a clean paint brush to coat the rose petals with the egg white, covering them fully on both sides.

Dip the petals in the sugar, using your hand or a teaspoon to douse them, ensuring they are fully coated.

Set on a wire rack to dry fully – for 3–4 hours or overnight. The crystallised petals will keep for a few weeks in a sealed container.

HONEYCOMB

PREP: 10 minutes
MAKES: around 150 g (5 oz)
of honeycomb

100 g (3½ oz/scant ½ cup)
caster (superfine) sugar

50g (2 oz/scant ¼ cup) golden
(light corn) syrup

1 tsp bicarbonate of soda
(baking soda)

flaky sea salt (optional)

Few things smell as inviting as a freshly made batch of honeycomb. While this isn't up to a postal journey by itself, it can be used in my Honeycomb + Milk Chocolate Biscuit Cake (page 56) or simply enjoyed at home as it is. The below recipe makes a small quantity (enough for the biscuit cake) but can easily be scaled up.

Line a small tin or tuppaware container with baking parchment, including the sides.

Place the sugar and golden syrup in a saucepan and set over a medium heat. Allow to fully melt, then turn up the heat and cook until the caramel is a deep amber colour.

Remove from the heat and immediately add the bicarbonate of soda and whisk in until foaming. Quickly pour into the lined tin (the mistake people often make is not getting it in the tin quick enough and loosing too much air). Sprinkle with sea salt, then allow to cool before breaking up and using.

ROYAL ICING

PREP: 10 minutes
MAKES: enough royal icing
to ice a Christmas Cake (page 83)
or a batch of vanilla or ginger
biscuits (pages 144 and 146)

2 egg whites

500 g (1 lb 2 oz/4 cups)
icing (confectioner's) sugar

1 tsp liquid glucose

1 tbsp lemon juice
(plus extra if needed)

gel food colouring (optional)

Royal icing is something of a classic in the baking world, and for good reason. It sets solid and pipes beautifully, making it the perfect choice for decorating.

Use the recipe below to pipe outlines onto biscuits. If you wish to flood them to cover fully, add a teaspoon of water to the remaining icing to loosen it, then use it to fill the centre of the piped space.

In the bowl of a stand mixer with a whisk attached, whisk the egg whites until they are foamy, but not yet forming peaks. Sift in the icing sugar and fold through the egg whites to combine. Add the glucose and lemon juice and mix through. If needed, add extra lemon juice or water – a teaspoon at a time – to get to the desired thick-but-pipeable consistency.

If you are colouring your icing, divide it between as many small bowls as you have colours and add a dab of gel colouring to each, mixing until you have an even colour.

Decant the icing into piping bags and tie firmly if posting.

INDEX

ACKNOWLEDGEMENTS

Writing a cookbook has been a dream ever since I was making bright green peppermint creams all those years ago. I am more thankful than I can say to have been given this opportunity – thank you to Kate Pollard for trusting in this idea and making it possible, and to Nassima Rothacker, Rosie Reynolds, Lauren Miller, Lucy Turnbull, Emma Burnett, Beth Bishop and Claire Warner for bringing it to life. Working with a group of such talented women has been the biggest privilege.

To my mum, Kathy, and grannies, Sue and Pam – thank you for making baking part of life from the beginning. It has truly been the greatest gift. To my dad, Mike, grandad, Ted and brothers William and Michael for proofreading and just generally being the most invested, kind and patient support network. I am very lucky to have you all.

Jess Collins, thank you for being such a brilliant friend and holding my hand on the first shoot day (and, frankly, every day).

To those of you over the years who tolerated total kitchen domination – particularly Rob Graham, Bethan Smyth and Tor Thomas – and my incredible network of testers, tasters and cheerleaders – chiefly Kate Robins, Emily Cropper, Ellie Boote, Beth Corbet, Alexandra Withers, Nancy Brownlow, Kate Downie, Sophie Macrae, Hannah Sprake, Patrick Buck, Mairi MacIver, Charlotte and Jason Baker, Laura Highton-Davidson, Grace Warman and Polly Scobie, thank you.

Thank you to Rochelle Cohen for supporting my extra-curricular baking ventures unreservedly, and for teaching me the value of hard work, high standards, and dogged determination.

Chris, you are truly my North Star. Thank you for riding the emotional rollercoaster, for embracing the off-cut life and for bringing me back to myself when I was a bit at sea. I am so lucky. Thank you for everything, F&A.

And last but by no means least, thank you to everyone who ordered postal treats and trusted me to bake for their loved ones. You kept me going through a global pandemic and without your support, this book would never have happened. I hope you enjoy baking these recipes as much as I loved writing them.

SPECIALIST SUPPLIERS

UK

Boxes, cellophane:
RAJA (www.rajapack.co.uk)

Tissue paper:
RAJA (www.rajapack.co.uk)
Floristry Warehouse (www.floristrywarehouse.com)

Ribbons & tape:
Floristry Warehouse (www.floristrywarehouse.com)
Etsy (www.etsy.co.uk) or any haberdashery –
John Lewis (www.johnlewis.com) carries a good
selection in store

Pressed flowers:
If you don't fancy pressing your own, I recommend
Nurtured In Norfolk (www.nurturedinnorfolk.co.uk)

Freeze dried fruit:
BRIX, available via Amazon

Edible gold and silver leaf: KINNO, available
via Amazon or Waitrose (www.waitrose.com)

USA

Boxes, cellophane:
Target (www.target.com)
Walmart (www.walmart.com)
Packaging Supplies (www.packagingsupplies.com)

Tissue paper:
Michaels (www.michaels.com)
Party Delights (www.partydelights.co.uk)

Ribbons & tape:
Michaels (www.michaels.com)
Paper Source (www.papersource.com)
Rifle Paper Co (www.riflepaperco.com)

Pressed flowers:
Etsy (www.etsy.com)
Idle Wild (www.idlewildfloral.com)

Freeze dried fruit:
Whole Foods (www.wholefoodsmarket.com)
Augason Farms or Glendee via Amazon

Edible gold and silver leaf:
Slo Food Group (www.slofoodgroup.com)

AUSTRALIA

Boxes, cellophane:
Oz Pack (www.ozpack.com.au)
New Pack (www.newpack.com.au)

Tissue paper:
Koch & Co (www.koch.com.au)

Ribbons:
Vandoros (www.vandoros.com.au)
The Party Parlour (www.thepartyparlour.com.au)

Pressed flowers:
Etsy (www.etsy.com/au)

Freeze dried fruit:
Gourmet Grocer Online
   (www.gourmetgroceronline.com.au)
Berry Fresh (www.berryfresh.com.au)

Edible gold and silver leaf:
Gold Leaf Factory (www.goldleaf.com.au)
Lollipop Cake Supplies
   (www.lollipopcakesupplies.com.au)

LUCY BURTON

Lucy is a London-based baker and recipe writer who runs a bespoke wedding cake business alongside her work as a hospitality PR director. Her recipes and cakes have featured in *The Telegraph*, *Hello! Magazine*, *OK! Magazine* and *You & Your Wedding*, and her postal cakes business was lauded by the *Financial Times* and *Town & Country Magazine*. She lives in Stoke Newington, North London.

@lucyburtonbakes

Published in 2022 by OH Editions
Part of Welbeck Publishing Group.
Based in London and Sydney.
www.welbeckpublishing.com

Design © 2022 OH Editions

Text © 2022 Lucy Burton
Photography © 2022 Nassima Rothacker

A CIP catalogue record for this book is available
from the British Library.

ISBN UK 978-1-91431-728-6
ISBN US 978-1-91431-753-8

Publisher: Kate Pollard
Editor: Dan Hurst
Designer: Claire Warner Studio
Prop stylist: Lauren Miller
Production controller: Arlene Alexander

Printed and bound by RR Donnelley in China

MIX
Paper from
responsible sources
FSC® C144853
FSC
www.fsc.org

10 9 8 7 6 5 4 3 2 1